gaytimes

Amsterdam

John Szponarski

Absolute Press

First published in Great Britain
in 2002 jointly by:

Absolute Press
Scarborough House
29 James Street West
Bath BA1 2BT
Phone 44 (0) 1225 316013
Fax 44 (0) 1225 445836
E-mail
info@absolutepress.demon.co.uk
Website
www.absolutepress.demon.co.uk

Gay Times Books
an imprint of Millivres Ltd
part of
Millivres Prowler Group
Worldwide House
116-134 Bayham Street
London NW1 0BA
Website
www.gaytimes.co.uk

Contributing editors:
Martin Wood (Museums, Shops)
Andy Dixon (Restaurants)

A catalogue record of this book is available from the British Library

ISBN 1 899791 49 3

Printed and bound in Italy by
Lego Print

Every effort has been made to ensure that the facts in this book are accurate and up-to-date. It is still recommended that travellers obtain advice and information from airlines, switchboards, etc. about current travel and accommodation requirements and from clubs and venues to ensure that details have not changed since this book went to print. The author and publishers cannot accept any responsibility for inconvenience, injury or loss resulting from the information herein.

Contents

Also available
Gay Times Great Britain and Ireland
Gay Times London

Gay Times

The most trusted name in gay publishing. At last, guides for the independent holidaymaker that are thoroughly researched and regularly updated, by lesbians and gay men who know each destination as well as you know your home town. Each book will detail and demystify the local scene and explore the lifestyle, attractions and history that frame it.

Co-publishers Absolute Press are responsible for the gay biography imprint, *Outlines*. Together with Gay Times they have already published the most thorough guide to Great Britain and Ireland available. This series will grow to include guide books to the key destinations across the world. It sets a new standard of excellence in gay travel guide publishing.

The author

John Szponarski has lived and travelled across Britain and Ireland for much of his life. Occasional forays from his Manchester home have come as a pleasant distraction from the domestic confines of his otherwise sober life. This year he has been busy, simultaneously compiling the *London* and *Amsterdam* guides, under the illusion that travel expenses would allow him the luxury of digressing from the project in hand. They didn't. John begrudgingly delivered two new titles to add to his acclaimed *Great Britain and Ireland*, that got the series rolling last year. Still not recognised, by name or face, still having to pay on the door and shout drinks at the bar (despite insistent introductions) and still befriending unsuspecting members of the opposite sexual persuasion, John goes about his work with a quiet dedication. His is one of the most intelligent and refreshing gay voices writing on the scene today.

Acknowledgments
As always, my first acknowledgement of sincere thanks goes to my friend and colleague Matt Inwood of Absolute Press. His sheer dedication knows no bounds and I am proud that my work is always associated with his name. I also acknowledge the support of my dearest and closest friends David, Paul and Martin. Finally, my thanks go to Pieter and Seb, my two personal Dutch escorts who over the years have made my stay in their home and country so welcoming. My thanks to the publisher, Jon Croft, and the Managing Director of Millivres-Prowler Group, Simon Topham, for having faith in this project. Finally, I wholeheartedly thank the many readers of the previous guides for taking the time to convey in writing their thoughts and comments. I have given them my consideration in tackling this new guide.

Foreword

The Venice of the North.
The Gayway to Europe.
Call it what you will, Amsterdam is stunning, and Amsterdam is gay. Its history dates back to the thirteenth century, when inhabitants dammed the Amstel, thereby giving the city its name. Today, it stands proud as an international seat of business, and as one of the richest cultural centres and most tolerant and accepting cities in the world.

Millions of visitors pour into this city every year. Many hundreds of thousands of these visitors are gay, for there is an exciting, eclectic and liberal air to the city that is almost tangible. When you are staggering back to your hotel and you don't get that uneasy feeling of being in a strange city – you can only be in Amsterdam. More than anywhere in the world, this is a city where you can flaunt and enjoy your sexuality freely.

Essentials

Getting there

When to go

Millions of visitors pour into Amsterdam every year, right across the seasons. In the middle of summer, the sky is still light as late as 2300. This suits such a laid-back city – many shops open their doors at around 1000 in the morning, and bars and cafés stay open late through the night and into the following morning, until 0100 or 0200. Amsterdam's climate is relatively mild, and rarely soars or dips beyond this norm. The Netherlands is a flat country, though, and this does make for changeable weather which means that days can start off seemingly bleak but perk up into sunshine in the afternoon, and vice versa. The city sees a fair amount of rain throughout the year, especially in winter, so prepare yourself for showers. The worst of winter might amount to the odd freeze here or there, though rarely accompanied by snow, whereas the best of summer can see temperatures peaking at just over 25° Celsius and people festooned across every nook and cranny of city park and stretch of canal.

What to take

Pack **clothing** that will cope with for the unpredictable weather patterns mentioned above. A few warm woollies if your visit should fall between October and April, with rain hood or umbrella a desirable accessory. In the summer, you might want to make sure you've got a couple of items that finish above the knee (although beware of mosquitoes along the canals). Your inclination might be to explore the city via a relaxing canal cruise, if, however, you fancy doing as the locals do, then you will probably want to hire a bike whilst you are over here, so make sure you bring a sturdy pair of training shoes with you.

The **voltage** in the Netherlands is 220-230V/50 Hz (the European standard) but travellers from North America are advised to bring a power converter (which changes the voltage) and an adapter (to change the shape of the plug) for two-prong, round-pin plugs. If you do forget to bring one, there is no need to worry. Many shops around the centre will sell them for around €7. Do not make the mistake of only using an adaptor. If you are not sure ask a professional. Tourists from the EU, New Zealand, South Africa and Australia will not need to convert the voltage. Try to avoid bringing over electrical items unless you need to: most hotels will be able to provide you with the basics from radio alarms to hairdryers.

If you need to bring **prescribed medicines or pharmaceutical products** into the country, then these need to be transported in their original containers (preferably in your hand baggage with the container seals intact) and the contents clearly marked. A letter from your doctor should also be carried, along with details of the generic names of the prescription in case you need to obtain a further supply from a Dutch doctor. If your condition is chronic or severe, then the letter from your doctor should carry detailed information in order to expedite your treatment.

Regulations regarding the **carriage of animals** are complex and vary from country to country and airline to airline. You should contact the animal welfare authorities in Amsterdam and you should also seek advice from your airline or a specialist pet travel agency before planning your journey. Airlines will only carry animals if advance arrangements have been made, as space is very often limited. There are three available options for airlines that will allow you to take pets. Your airline will be able to tell you which services they can offer: (i) as carry-on baggage: some airlines will accept very small animals as carry-on baggage, providing the container will fit under a seat. The animal will not be permitted to be taken out of the container during the flight; (ii) as accompanied baggage: most airlines will accept animals as accompanied baggage providing they are in a suitable container and they will travel in the baggage compartment where a suitable environment can be maintained (note: animals arriving in the UK may only do so as manifested air cargo); (iii) as air cargo: owners can arrange for their animals to travel as air cargo without making the journey themselves. Arrangements for ferries and trains should be checked ahead of travelling or when making the booking.

Required paperwork

European Union (EU) nationals and citizens of Australia, Canada, United States and New Zealand need only a valid passport to visit the Netherlands. This is provided that your stay is for less than three months for either business or pleasure. If you intend to stay longer you should get your passport stamped on entry to the country and have in your possession a residence permit.

Customs and excise

Since July 1999, duty-free goods have been unavailable for EU nationals. However, even if you are paying duty on your purchases you will find that the low tax burden in the Netherlands can offer you impressive savings on items like tobacco and alcohol. For example, 200 cigarettes bought in the UK can cost as much as €78 (£47) while purchasing the same quantity from the airport shops in Amsterdam, including the tax paid, will cost you in the region of €32 (£20). And, as the tax has been paid, there is no limit to the amount you can bring in as long as it is 'for your own use'. There are guidelines to quantify the amount that is acceptable for your own use, and these are, per person, as follows: 10 litres of spirits, 800 cigarettes, 90 litres of wine, 110 litres of beer.

Non-EU citizens flying home from Amsterdam can buy duty-free goods although the limits are severely restricted to around 1 litre of alcohol and 200 cigarettes. If you pay duty on them, then there is no limitation within reasonable limits. Those interested in pursuing some tulip growing of their own once home might want to have their bulbs posted back by the vendor – many of the reputable outlets in Amsterdam offer this service at a reasonable extra cost and complete all the necessary paperwork.

Arriving into Amsterdam

Amsterdam is served by one of the largest railway terminals in Europe, Centraal Station, and it's easy to get there from all the major cities in Europe. The train journey from London via Brussels by Eurostar (www.eurostar.com) takes six to seven hours. You can also reach

Amsterdam from the UK and Norway by ferry. However, for sheer speed and convenience, most visitors to Amsterdam arrive by air at one of the world's busiest and best airports. Book far enough in advance, travel midweek and hunt around and you should find plenty of bargain flights on these highly competetive routes.

Amsterdam Schiphol Airport (AMS)

Amsterdam Schiphol Airport Phone 350 3308
All planes arrive at Schiphol airport which is situated about nine miles (14 km) south-west of the centre of Amsterdam. Schiphol's one terminal is built around a huge central plaza that incorporates dozens of shops, restaurants, duty-free (and duty-paid) See, Buy, Fly outlets and even a couple of sushi bars. There is talk of a brothel being a permanent fixture at the airport although this 'world first' has been speculated upon for a number of years. A branch of the **VVV** (**tourist information**) is based in the plaza and offers a hotel reservation service, although the constant, long queues can make the process quite daunting. The centre is open Monday to Sunday, from 0700 until 2200. There are several bureaux de change, most of them in the plaza and arrivals hall, plus exchange machines which can change 37 different currencies into euros. There is also a 24-hour GWK currency exchange branch in the plaza. The **lost property office** (601 2443) is in the basement between arrival lounges 1 and 2 and is open Monday to Friday between 0730 and 1730, and Saturday to Sunday between 0900 and 1700. Elevators down to the railway station beneath the terminal are located in the plaza.

Schiphol into central Amsterdam

By train: Trains depart from the airport station (usually platform 3 beneath the central plaza) for the 20-minute journey to **Amsterdam Centraal Station** (CS) every 15 minutes from 0400 until 2400, and then hourly through the night from 0045 until 0400. A single ticket costs €2.90, available from the vast ranks of ticket offices situated on the central plaza in the airport itself. Signs in English on the window of each counter direct you to the correct platform. When you arrive in Amsterdam and emerge from Centraal Station, you will be on Stationsplein. From here, you can get a taxi or tram to your hotel or apartment or, if reasonably central, you can walk. If you are planning to walk, remember to pack a simple foldaway luggage trolley that can be accessed once you reach the station. Keep an eye on your luggage at all times. The railway system from the airport to the station is rife with thieves and pickpockets.

By shuttle: A convenient **KLM shuttle service** (653 4975) takes passengers from the airport to many city-centre hotels with stops at Leidseplein, Westmarkt-Keizerfracht, Dam Square, Nieuwezijds Voorburgwal, Zeedijk and then returning to Schiphol airport. This service is available to everyone whether you are staying at the hotel where the shuttle stops or not. There are two different routes: Route A makes mainly central stops; and Route B mainly southern stops. Check on the board by the stop to determine which shuttle will take you nearest to your destination. Double-check with the driver if you are still unsure. The one-way fare for this service is in the region of €8. It departs every 20 minutes from outside the plaza entrance from 0600 until 2000 and then every half hour until 2300.

By taxi: All taxis operate from the taxi rank at the front of the plaza, but taking a taxi to the city centre is expensive and by no means convenient. The trains depart regularly and it is easier to get to the railway platforms than it is to the taxi ranks. If your final destination is well out of the city centre or lugging your heavily laden cases (packed with rubber waders and hoods) is just not practical on public transport, then you'll probably need to take a taxi. Allow for a fare in the region of €25-30 and a journey time of about 30 minutes to get to your destination. For information, reservations or fares phone **Taxicentrale** (653 1000).

Airline information

Once you have arrived in Amsterdam, it's a good idea to have to hand the number of the airline just in case you lose your outgoing ticket, or are in danger of missing your flight. In such instances, you will need to contact the airline quickly, and, as with your passport, have photocopies all travelling documents to speed up your enquiry. Here are some of the major operators.

Aer Lingus (601 0265)
Aeroflot (627 0561)
Air France (446 8800)
Air Holland (316 4444)
Alitalia (474 7747)
Austrian Airlines (627 7144)
British Airways (346 9559)
British Midland (662 2211)
Cathay Pacific (653 2010)
China Airlines (646 1001)
Continental Airlines (346 9381)
Cyprus Airways (653 3546)
Delta Airlines (504 0606)
Easyjet(568 4880)
Egyptair (625 6661)
El Al Israel Airlines (644 0101)
Japan Airlines (305 0060)
KLM Royal Dutch Airlines (474 7747)
LOT Polish Airlines (616 9266)
Lufthansa (582 9456)
Malaysia Airlines (626 2420)
Northwest Airlines (474 7747)
Olympic Airways (405 7215)
PIA Pakistan International (626 4715)
SAS Scandinavian (454 6500)

Singapore Airlines (548 8800)

Swiss Air Lines (679 5000)

TAP Air Portugal (638 7276))

Turkish Airlines (685 3801)

United Airlines (504 0555)

Getting about

Amsterdam has an extensive, cheap and efficient public transport system with the tram, rather than the metro, being the form of transport most relevant to the tourist. Unless you are planning on visiting districts outside the centre of Amsterdam, the tramline you will most likely use will be line 20, the Circle line (see below). This very busy line will take you to most of the sights and areas of importance to the gay tourist. The metro and bus system is good for getting you to areas outside the city although it is unlikely you will ever have to use these forms of transport if you are just visiting the city itself.

One of the first places you should visit is the **GVB office** (public transport company) on Stationsplein or the GVB central office at Prins Hendrikkade 108-114. Here, you can make travel enquiries, pick up free transport maps and timetables and purchase tickets for all forms of public transport. The Stationsplein office is open from Monday to Sunday, 0700 until 2230.

By tram

Most tramlines route from Centraal Station to the city areas in the east (oost), south (zuid) and west (west). The others mutually connect these city areas. An exception is line 20A and 20B, the Circle tram that runs through the city centre, with Centraal Station as both beginning and end of the line. Tram 20 is the ideal way to get an overview of the heart of the city, passing some of the city's most famous sights. Remember to board at either the east side (20A) or the west side (20B) depending on which direction you wish to go. The Circle tram only runs through the day, departing every 12 to 15 minutes from 0900 until 1900 from Centraal Station. The first trip departs at 0900 and the last at 1800. This applies to both directions. If you are going to use this tram as your main means of getting around it would be in your interest to purchase a Circle tram ticket for either one day (€5.20), two days (€6.60), three days (€8.40) or four days (€10.20). These tickets are also valid on all other forms of public transport within the same time period. You can also purchase a *strippenkaart*, the smallest (€6.00) consisting of 15 'strips'. When you enter the tram you have to punch your card depending on how many zones you plan to go through. For example, much of Amsterdam's centre is in Zone 1, so punch your card twice (using two strips); if you are going into Zone 2, punch your card three times, and so on. If you are confused ask someone – they are usually helpful. Once you stamp your card it is valid for an hour so you can use the tram as often as you like within this period of time without stamping your card again. Do not try to dodge paying the fare – line 20 has a permanent conductor on board and other forms of transport using the honesty system have frequent ticket inspections. The on-the-spot fine for fare dodging is €30.

Always board the tram from the rear and punch your ticket in the machine to validate your pass. The driver, and more often than not a conductor, will also be able to validate your pass. Apart from Line 20, the trams run from Monday to Friday from 0600 to 0000, Saturday from 0630 to 0000 and Sunday from 0730 to 0000.

Line 20A – route of the circle tram:
Centraal Station (east side), Dam, Spui, Muntplein, Rembrandtsplein, Waterlooplein, Mr Visserplein, Plantage Parklaan, Plantage Kerklaan, Nieuwe Keizersgracht, Roetersstraat, Weesperplein, Oosteinde, Frederiksplein, Stadhouderskade, van Woustraat, 2e van der Helststraat, Ferdinand Bolstraat, Ruysdaelkade, Roelof Hartplein, Museumplein, van Baerlestraat, Hobbemastraat, Leidseplein, Raamplein, Elandsgracht, Marnixstraat, Westermarkt, Dam, Nieuwezijds Kolk, Martelaarsgracht, Centraal Station (west side).

By bus

For the majority of tourists staying in Amsterdam there will be little need to use the bus service as the trams do more than an efficient job of getting you from one side of town to the other. However, once the trams stop at night the bus service comes into its own, running from 0100 to 0530, Monday through to Friday, and until 0630 over the weekends. Night buses are numbered from 71 to 79, all going to and from Centraal Station, except 79. Night bus stops are indicated by a black square at the stop with the bus number printed on it. For details on all bus services and current timetables visit the GVB office on Stationsplein.

By train

Visitors who intend to stay in the city of Amsterdam for the duration of their trip will find little reason to use the railway service. That doesn't mean to say that Centraal Station itself holds no delights! For the architecturally savvy person, this palatial 1800s construction is the largest railway terminal in the world. The station might also be worth mooching around if you're after 'a bit of the other' – the rear of the station and the intermittent archways in the foyer hold opportunity of sex for sale in the form of rent boys. Adventurous sorts fill the concourses too, for from here you can access many parts of the Netherlands and, of course, Europe. You need only to purchase your ticket from the main office at the front of the station (remember that travel on international trains always requires a reservation).

By metro

The underground system in Amsterdam is a combination of full metro and rapid trams (sneltram) running mainly on the surface, with only 3.5 kilometres of track in the city centre between Centraal Station and Amstel actually being underground. Unless you are planning to visit districts out of the city it is highly unlikely that you will be using the metro system. If you are, call in at the **GVB** on Stationsplein or the tourist information office and pick up a free map of the metro (Snelwijzer) and a current timetable.

By taxi

Taxis in Amsterdam are a rather expensive means of travel with a boarding charge of €2.20 plus €1.54 per kilometre travelled. They are not supposed to stop if hailed in the street, although it does happen. Instead, they are supposed to queue up at designated ranks (to be found at Centraal Station, the bus station at Kinkerstraat and Marnixstraat, Rembrandtplein and Leidseplein). You can't pre-book a taxi for a certain time but you can phone for one for immediate use. Bear in mind, however, that weekends are particularly busy periods and even getting through on the phone can be frustrating. You are quite likely to be placed in a queue whilst waiting for the taxi operator to answer your call, with a Dalek-sounding voice pronouncing, *Er zijn nog drie... een, twee or drie* (caller number one, two or three) indicating how many people there are in front of you in the electronic queue. As for the journey itself, it is rare to be overcharged but if you believe you have been ripped off make sure you get a receipt from the driver, make a mental note about the direction taken, pick-up and destination points and phone the taxi company concerned. There are two taxi firms that serve the city: **Taxicentrale Amsterdam** (677 7777), **Taxi Direkt** (0900 0724).

By bike

As flat as Amsterdam is, you've no reason not to do as the locals do and get around the city on a bike. The city has a large network of bicycle lanes to facilitate any two-wheeled excursion you might have in mind. Bike theft in the city is high, so be sure never to leave your bike without well-securing it to some immovable object. Renting bikes is simple and relatively cheap, so go on, join in with everyone else.

By canal boat

Would you go to Venice and not travel down its canals? No, well nor should you shirk the opportunity in Amsterdam. Its the best vantage point from which to see much of the city and to judge the lay of the land. If you're going to take a cruise, you'd be well-advised to take it early or late in the day as the canals do tend to get rather congested during the middle hours. **Amsterdam Canal Cruises** (626 5636) offer a good tour of the city's waterways.

On foot

A good pair of walking shoes or trainers will take you a long way in Amsterdam. The city is small enough to explore on foot and the wealth of side streets, shops and places to stop off at mean that this could be the most hassle-free way of getting around.

Getting by

Currency

A member of the European Union (EU), the Netherlands gave up the guilder and adopted the euro (€) on 1 January 2002 for all monetary transactions. Euro notes come in denominations of 5, 10, 20, 50, 100, 200 and the rather awkwardly large 500. Each euro is divided into 100 cents. Coins are issued in denominations of 1, 2, 5, 10, 20 and 50 cents. It will be rare for you to see or be issued with 1- and 2-cent pieces as they are practically worthless. Plans are afoot to soon introduce €1 and €2 coins. It is extremely hard or nigh-on impossible to change €500 notes at many shops or venues. In order to avoid this pending hassle, refuse to accept such a large denomination note and ask for something smaller – €100 should be large enough for most out-and-about occasions.

At the time of writing, the euro had an average value, over a three-month period, of £0.63 against the British pound sterling.

Bureaux de change

As in most international cities it is better to use the tried and tested financial institutions and avoid street kiosks offering money exchange services as their charges may not always be readily and easily understood. Remember, *verkoopt* means sell, while *koopt* means buy. Keep an eye on the rate before you travel and jump at the most favourable rate you can. Travellers' cheques are always a safe form of currency, but will not suffice for every eventuality. There are several reputable bureaux in the city: **Thomas Cook** at Dam 23-25 (625 0922), surprisingly, has a reputation for a rather high commission rate; **Post Office (PTT)** at Singel 250 offers a good exchange rate; **GWK** is a national organisation with currency exchange offices at Centraal Station, the airport among other locations, and offer fairly good exchange rates and, in some offices, 24-hour service; **Change Express** Damrak 86 (624 6681) with whom you should be careful to check the commission and service charge rates; and good ol' **American Express** at Damrak 66 (520 7777). Those Brits who yearn for familiar surroundings and a cup of tea before exchanging their money can head for the currency exchange desk at Marks & Spencer at Kalverstraat 66-72.

Travellers' cheques

These will prevent you carrying excessive amounts of cash around and if they are stolen or lost you can usually replace them within 24 hours. They are widely accepted and easily exchanged at any of the banks in the city but to avoid additional exchange rate charges, you should be careful to have them made out in euros.

ATMs

This is the most convenient and cost-effective way of obtaining money. Check (before you leave home) that your bank card is programmed for overseas withdrawals and enquire as to what charges, if any, your bank will be making. Using ATMs means you can usually withdraw up to €200 per day at minimal cost. Cards with the Maestro symbol shouldn't have any difficulties in Amsterdam's machines.

Unlike in the United States, ATM machines in Europe do not have the alphabetic key indicators. If you are used to remembering your PIN number as letters, rather than as numbers, then it would be wise to memorise the numerical equivalent. Also, if your PIN is longer than four digits, check with your bank whether you are able to use just the first four numbers, or whether you will need a new card. The following list relates the numbers to their corresponding letters: 1 (QZ); 2 (ABC); 3 (DEF); 4 (GHI); 5 (JKL); 6 (MNO); 7 (PRS); 8 (TUV); 9 (WXZ). Remember you have only three attempts at punching your PIN correctly before the machine swallows your card!

Lost or stolen bank/credit cards

You should immediately report lost or stolen bank/credit cards to both the relevant agency and the police. The following numbers are for the main credit card distribution agencies.

American Express 504 8666

Diners Club 0800 0334 (toll free) or (010) 458 6105

Visa 660 0611 **or** Head Office 660 0600

Mastercard and Eurocard 283 5555 or Utrecht (030) 283 5777

Sales tax (BTW)

A 19-per-cent sales tax called Belasting Toegevoegde Waarde (BTW) is included in most prices (6 per cent on restaurant bills and 5 per cent on hotel bills). This tax is similar to VAT or GST, and travellers from non-EU countries can claim a refund on items over €135 if they are taken out of the EU within three months. You will need to get an export certificate from the shop that sells you the goods and get this endorsed by the customs official when you leave the EU. The customs officials will then send the stamped document back to the store who will then post you a cheque. An easier option is to shop at a place displaying a 'Tax Free for Tourists' sign on the window. Once you have made your purchases at these stores (over €135) the cashier will give you a stamped cheque that you can cash when you leave the EU. There are some exclusions to this scheme, such as gemstones and goods that require an export licence, but nothing that should affect you as a tourist purchasing souvenirs or gifts.

Lost property

Before leaving your home country you should make copies of the data page of your passport leaving one copy at home with someone whom you can call in an emergency, and one copy somewhere safe in your luggage, separate from your passport. In the event of loss or theft, report it immediately to the nearest police station ensuring you get an incident or report number. Report it also to your embassy or consulate at home. The production of your copy passport will make the process much easier and could save you at least a whole week in lost time.

If it's travellers' cheques that you have lost you then you need to check the wallet that they came in for information on how to report them lost or stolen. This is assuming that you still have the wallet! Don't be caught out: as with your passport and travelling documents, it is best to reproduce this information and keep it secure.

If you are a victim of theft during your time in the city you will need to report it to the **Police Headquarters** at Elandsgracht 117 (559 9111). You will be expected to give as much information as possible, such as the exact location at which the theft probably occurred, what items were stolen, their precise value, and so on. You will also be quizzed as to why on earth it happened to *you*, why *you* were not careful with your belongings, why *you* didn't ensure *your* belongings were adequately secured and so on. Don't expect sympathy. It was, after all, *your own* fault! Keep your wits about you.

If you happen to lose or leave behind any items on the trains then you can visit or call **Centraal Station Lost Property** at Stationsplein 15 (557 8544). Items found are kept for only four days before being sent to a sorting depot in Utrecht. If you've missed this window, you will need to phone Utrecht on (030) 235 3923. If the tram, bus or metro is the transport that witnessed your misfortune then contact **GVB Lost Property** at Prins Hendrikkade 108-114 (460 5858). If you've mislaid luggage at the airport then your journey really has got off to a bad start. **Schiphol Airport Lost Luggage** (649 1433) is the place to start your enquiries. If you're misfortunate enough to leave behind your jewels or gels in a taxi, then you will need to contact the taxi firm direct, so be sure to take note of the cab you're in. Finally, for any items lost in the street (or if you are just hopelessly lost) your ultimate port of call will be **Police Lost Property** at Stephensonstraat 18 (559 3005).

Street crime

On the whole, Amsterdam is a safe place to walk around, day or night, without fear of what might happen to you. But, like any major international city, it does have little pockets of crime where extra vigilance and care will be required. Notable areas are particularly Centraal Station, the red-light district and the multitude of streets popular with tourists, where pickpocketing and theft is rife. The police and tourist authority are well aware of, and embarrassed by, the growth of this sort of crime and the police intermittently reminds all of the need to be aware of pickpockets. It's not unusual, at festivals or street parties, for the police to bring along huge inflatables of characters being robbed with warnings to beware pickpockets. Banners are hung across many of the most touristy streets reiterating this advice. Despite the warnings, it continues to happen (probably whilst you're wearing a beguiled smile staring at huge inflatable police issue). Keep your eyes peeled.

A particularly lucrative trick of the pickpocket is to sidle up close to you and offer to sell you something illicit. Being in Amsterdam, this probably won't strike you as too unusual. Whilst you concentrate on what they are offering, or try to discourage them, they could be trying to rob you. Another well-known trick, and one that many hotel owners are keen to alert you to, is allowing someone to enter the hotel premises just as you are leaving through a secure door. The con artist will lead you to believe that he or she is another guest staying at the apartment complex or hotel. Should this happen, you are advised to inform them of the correct procedure of entering the building, via either their own key or through reception. Genuine guests will appreciate your caution whilst con artists will make a song and dance about it. Other opportunist con artists might approach you with their hard luck stories of being robbed, or having lost their wallet or any number of other reasons where they hope to make you feel guilty and thus provide financial help. Do not be taken in.

Mugging and assault do not occur often in Amsterdam. That is not to say that it can't happen to you if you don't keep your wits about you. Some of the streets that criss-cross the city can be deserted at night, providing a thief or mugger the ideal situation to commit a crime. If there are two or more of you your chances of being assaulted will be reduced. Single people should do their best to stick to well-lit main thoroughfares wherever they possibly can. One of the most lucrative periods of the year for petty theft is during Gay Pride. The streets and squares are so packed that being pushed and man-handled is par for the course. These festivals provide fertile ground for pick pockets and bag-snatchers and they'll take full opportunity of relieving you of your belongings. Do not keep your wallet in your back pocket.

Getting settled

For a major city Amsterdam is fairly compact and getting from one gay area to the other is relatively easy. The city is laid out in a series of concentric horseshoe-like shapes with Centraal Station being at the open end. Knowing how far away from the station you are will help guide you around the city in relative fashion and avoid you getting lost. The innermost canal bounding the station is the Singel, which terminates at Muntplein before carrying on as Kloveniersburgwal, leading back to the station. The next three canals are the big three: the Herengracht, the Keizersgracht and, the most outward canal, the Prinsengracht. The area between these last three canals is known as the Canal Ring (or belt) that contains the multitude of the city's nightlife and bars. The Canal Ring West is the area that is still bounded by the Herengracht, the Keizersgracht and the Prinsengracht north of the Leidseplein. Further out, lie the more residential neighbourhoods of Amsterdam – the Jordaan (to the west), the Plantage and the Jodenbuurt (to the east) and De Pijp (to the south).

Unlike many other cities in Europe and North America, there is no such thing as a ghettoised gay village in Amsterdam. All the gay venues coexist in complete harmony with many of their straight counterparts. However, there are five main recognised areas in the city that can be classified as 'known gay areas', a title that serves only to distinguish the parts of the city where a collection of gay venues are traditionally based. These areas are all within easy walking distance of each other and each has its own unique atmosphere.

Warmoesstraat This is known as the leather, fetish and darkroom area of Amsterdam. Many, but not all, of the leather bars and associated clubs are located in this street. The area was the original settlement of the city – a collection of wattle and daub cottages until the sixteenth century when the area was favoured by the rich merchants and powerful bankers. Thomas Nugent, a seasoned traveller, once wrote that Warmoesstraat is the only street where 'you are most likely to find English inns and so avoid being cheated by wily Dutchmen'. Oh, how times have changed! Today, it is a gateway into the infamous red-light district, an area occupying a series of maze-like side streets that radiate out from Oudezijds Voorburgwal canal.

Reguliersdwars-straat This is the mouthful of a street that sits quietly behind the Bloemmarkt and joins Rembrandtplein to Koningsplein. For the sake of a descriptive term, this could most accurately be described as the 'trendy' gay area. Here lie some of the bars and clubs – such as Soho, Exit and April – that cater to the label-conscious men and women of the community who like to see and be seen.

Amstel

Another so-called trendy gay area, neighbouring on the opposite side of Rembrandtplein, based around the Amstel canal. This area is more open-plan than the others, offering the opportunity to sit and people-watch on the numerous terraces and patios. You can also locate the Paardenstraat in this area (rent boys!).

Kerkstraat

This is probably the oldest and most established gay area of the city. It takes in the expanse of space bounded by the Keizersgracht canal and the Prinsengracht canal, near to the Leidseplein. Here you will find the Thermos Night sauna and the Bronx hotel and sex shop, amongst numerous other gay venues.

Prinsengracht

The Prinsengracht canal leads from Centraal Station to join the Amstel and it has a number of gay venues leading off its thoroughfare around the straight Leidseplein area. The most notable of these venues is the Thermos Day sauna, as well as a number of gay hotels and café-bars.

Accommodation

In the city there is a raft of budget accommodation – most of the rooms in this category will be clean and comfortable but the standard of room furnishings and facilities will be bordering on the basic. In short, like everything else in life, you get what you pay for! There is another, more luxurious end to the accommodation scale, of course, with no shortage of places to blow your money in style. Fortunately, the majority of gay and gay-friendly accommodation is good and the pervasive liberal atmosphere is one that extends to this industry, and your stay in the city as a gay, lesbian or same-sex couple should be pleasurable. The range of accommodation on offer results in a range of prices, and it can be well worth asking about discounts or the chance of hiring a cheap guest-bed for an accompanying friend.

Types of accommodation vary. You can lay your hat in a range of hotels, from the very basic, where prices start around the €50 mark, to the grandeur of five-star hotel complexes, such as the Krasnapolsky Hotel in Dam Square, at the heart of the city – one of the few places where one indulgent night could warrant one of those blasted €500 notes! Guest-houses, bed and breakfasts, canal boats and apartments to let are all available for reasonable rates.

Squats

A vibrant squat culture still exists in Amsterdam although it is not nearly as prolific as the heady days of the sixties and seventies. Laws are in place to deter property developers from purchasing buildings and allowing them to remain empty waiting for the price to increase. Thereby, anyone who is homeless can put to use a building if it has been left standing empty for a year and a day, providing it is furnished with a chair, a table and a mattress, and the occupier announces their intention to inhabit.

Some of the best underground dance parties are held in these squats. If you are interested, you can find out the current locations by searching the listings in *Shark*, a monthly, alternative listings guide for Amsterdam, distributed free at bars, cafés, coffeeshops and cultural centres throughout the city. The easiest place for visitors to pick it up is at the **AUB Ticket Office** on the corner of Leidseplein and Marnixstraat.

Language

English is spoken as second nature throughout Amsterdam and asking the question 'Do you speak English?' could prove insulting to some. 'Of course I do,' will likely come the reply. Almost all greetings are opened with a cheery *Hallo* or the Dutch version *Hoi*, and then continue in English. Still, making the effort to use manners – please (*alstublieft*) and thank you (*dank u wel*) – in the mother tongue is guaranteed to bring a smile to the recipient's face and will no doubt bring you better service.

Tipping

Tipping is commonplace throughout the Netherlands. Taxis will expect a ten-per-cent tip, particularly if they have helped with your luggage. Restaurants also expect a ten-per-cent tip although make sure that a service charge is not already included on the bill. Bartenders do not really expect to be tipped on a single drink but if a large round has been pulled it is customary to round up the price to the nearest euro. Many clubs and venues have the services of a toilet attendant who will practically demand that you tip her (or him) at least €0.25 upon using the facilities. This is part of Dutch culture, so don't play the ignorant tourist – just pay the protection-racket-style tip. I once winced as the vile old woman in Club iT grabbed a young lad as he was leaving the toilet and verbally abused him for snubbing her dish. Needless to say, I put the little man away and readied my euros quickly.

Facts, foibles and fiddley customs

Apart from Centraal Station there are no other enclosed public toilet facilities in the city. This puts a stop to all cottaging and tea-room activities. Dotted throughout the city, particularly on major streets and down the canal arteries, are green metal or plasticised *pissoirs*. These are designed to accommodate up to four people at a time and only your water gun is shielded from the gaze of the passing public. This is fine for men, but women are very badly short-changed in the street-pissing stakes. A form of retaliation took place back in the seventies, when a group of feminists trying to draw attention to this blatant form of discrimination bound many of the pissoirs with swathes of pink ribbon. Some 30 years on and still there are no public facilities for women (except for one now newly installed at Sciphol). Popping into the nearest café or bar for a leak is acceptable practice although those in the centre do tend to employ the services of an attendant, so you may well have to pay for the privilege.

Much to the annoyance of many non-smoking tourists (the ones who pretend to cough and splutter at the merest sound of a match striking sandpapered strip), restaurants will allow their customers (the right) to smoke cigarettes whilst dining. You should not expect a smoke-free environment. Fast-food chains also have a considerable space set aside for smokers, usually denoted by the provision of ashtrays but always look for the 'Smoking

Area' signs prominently displayed in the buildings. Smoking is not allowed on public transport and in taxis, however, though some of the older Dutch residents still insist on lighting up regardless on the trams. Smoking cannabis outside coffeeshops is frowned upon although some bar and club owners do not mind. It is always best to enquire if you are not sure. Also, whilst in restaurants and other public auditoriums, it is polite to switch mobile phones off (or onto vibrate mode).

It would appear to be the national sport in Amsterdam for locals to see how many tourists they can knock down or maliciously clip with their Miss-Marple-type bikes! They can be very unforgiving of the unknowing tourist. You see, there is an etiquette to the city's cycle lanes and bicyclists tend to get a little miffed when they see that we don't follow – or care – for it. Don't give them the satisfaction of reprimanding you for jay-walking in their lanes (though they happily cut across all the bloody pavement!). Simply keep to your part of the road. Cycle lanes are designated with white lines.

And so to the city's official insignia – the three Xs – which appears everywhere. It represents the three virtues of charity, resolution, and heroism, and is not, as some may like to think, the hallmark of a city founded on sex. In 1489, as legend has it, the Holy Roman Emperor Maximilian I received medical assistance after falling ill in the city. After recovering, he showed his thanks by granting the city the right to use his insignia. Little could he have known that generations on it would be emblazoned across the most phallic-looking street furniture!

Getting help

Tourist information (VVV)

The **VVV** (**Vereniging voor Vreemdelingen Verkeer**) is the symbol of the Netherlands tourist association. The main office is **VVV Amsterdam Kantoor Stationsplein** at Aankomstpassage Schiphol Plaza 40 (open Monday to Sunday from 0700 to 2200) and there is a slightly smaller but busier office inside the station itself (open Monday to Saturday from 0900 to 2300, with reduced Easter hours). Another main office is **VVV Amsterdam Kantoor Leidseplein**, based on platform 1 (open Monday to Saturday from 0900 to 1700). From any of these offices you can get maps, travel information and details on all the major sights and excursions. If you are going there just to get a street map and the offices are busy with queues that just don't seem to be moving, they can be purchased for around €1.80-2 at a number of alternative places on the Damrak or at any of the souvenir shops. Inside the VVV there is also a bureau de change (although the exchange rates can be rather high) and the money-spinning room reservation and booking service. Pick up a free copy of *Amsterdam This Week* that's packed with information on sights and current events or purchase a copy of *Day and Night* for €1.50 which gives you the low-down on what's on around the city in a day-by-day format.

Pink Point of Presence (PPP)

Situated on Westermarkt next to the Homomonument on the corner of Keizersgracht and Radhuisstraat, is the PPP. Open between April and

September from Monday to Sunday, 1200 to 1800, this is a mobile information kiosk for gay and lesbian travellers, like a gay version of the VVV. The kiosk was introduced in 1998 as a store of information on gay happenings in Amsterdam. Unbelievably friendly staff will help you get your hands on free maps, leaflets and listings to the gay scene in Amsterdam. If the staff here don't know about a particular gay event then it is not worth knowing about. They also sell souvenir items which help to fund the project, such as postcards, T-shirts, and what-nots – all with a gay twist! From June to September, a walking tour on the history of gay life in the city departs from the PPP every Saturday at 1500. €18 per person. Well worth it.

Important numbers

All operators of emergency calls can speak English fluently. They can also converse in German and Italian. Calls to the emergency services – police, fire or ambulance – are free of charge. Just dial 112 and state the service you require. Calls to the operator number below are also free and the same number will get you through to both domestic and international services. Other numbers that I hope you won't need to use are the Legal Advice Line, which offers free advice from student solicitors and the Eerstelijn number for women victims of rape and assault.

Emergency 112

Operator (including collect calls) 0800 0410

Directory enquiries 0900 8008

Country code 31

Amsterdam Area Code 020

Tourist Medical Services 695 5638 (24 hour)

Police

If you find yourself on the other side of the law and the police have restrained you for one reason or another – being in possession of hard drugs (cocaine and heroin) is the popular 'bust' – then try to get in touch with your consulate as soon as you can. Surprisingly, Dutch police are not under any legal obligation to allow you a phone call and can detain you for up to 24 hours without charge. The main police headquarters are **Hoofdbureau van Politie** at Elandsgracht 117 (559 9111). You should call them with any non-emergency calls. If you are worried about a brush with the law or concerned that you might be about to break it the ring the **Legal Advice Line** (444 6333), which has a team of student solicitors that offer free advice. Finally, there is a helpline for women vistims of rape and sexual assault: **De Eerstelijn** (613 0245). If you are the victim of a homophobic assault then you must report it to the police. They will take your case seriously and they should be able to suggest an appropriate organisation if they feel that you need any extra support.

Medical services

Shit happens! And it will usually happen whilst you are on holiday. A broken tooth, food poisoning or a trip or fall. You can't foresee this sort of thing so you should be well prepared. If you are on prescriptive medication then heed the warning on page 11 of this guide. If carrying syringes or needles, be sure to carry a physician's letter documenting their medical necessity. Pack all medications in hand luggage as well as carrying a duplicate supply in the checked luggage. If you wear glasses or contacts, bring an extra pair. If you have significant allergies or chronic medical problems, wear a medical alert bracelet. It is infinitely better to be over prepared than otherwise. Pack a small emergency medical and dental kit – if you are going as part of a group then allocate these responsibilities to one person who is responsible enough to take charge in a medical crisis or emergency. Although Amsterdam will have numerous outlets that can provide you with medication and treatment, incidents will no doubt happen during the night or at other inconvenient times.

The Netherlands has a reciprocal health agreement with all other EU countries. On presentation of form **E111** medical treatment, including hospital treatment, is free. Prescribed medicines and dental treatment must, however, be paid for. Further information can be obtained from **Algemeen Nederlands Onderling Ziekenfonds** (the Netherlands General Sickness Insurance Fund) at Kaap Hoorndreef 24-28, Utrecht. Outside the EU, the Netherlands has reciprocal health agreements with Cape Verde, Morocco, Tunisia, Turkey, Serbia and Montenegro. All other travellers are advised to take out full medical insurance.

Central Medical Service (0900 503 2042)
A 24-hour service that will refer you to a duty practitioner

Central Medical Academy Meibergdreef 9 (566 9111)
For hospital care, situated near the Holendrecht metro stop

Centraal Doktorsdienst/Atacom (592 3434)
An NHS Direct type of phone service. English speakers who are trained to reassure and/or spot medical emergencies

Kruispost Oudezijds Voorburgwal 129 (624 9031)
For free emergency medical care weekdays only between 0645 and 2300

STD Clinic Groenburgwal 44 (622 3777)

STD Helpline (623 2252)

SOS Telephone Helpline (675 7575)
A Samaritans-type organisation for all kinds of emotional problems

If you desperately need to see a dentist (*tandart*) then the most useful number you can have about you is the 24-hour **Dental Administration Bureau** (0900 821 2230) who will be able to put you in touch with the nearest dentist able to cater for your oral needs. **TBB** (570 9595) is another 24-hour service – use them if you're in need of a dentist. They also have information about dispensing pharmacies. **AOC** Wilhelmina Gasthuisplein 167 (616 1234) also offer emergency dental care, and are open weekdays from 0900 to 1600.

If you have damaged your spectacles or mislaid your contact lenses then try the following centrally located opticians (*optiek*) to help you through this emergency: **York Optiek** Heiligeweg 8 (623 3295). They are open Monday to Friday from 0900 to 1800, and Saturday from 0930 to 1700.

Late-night chemists

There are two types of pharmacy in Amsterdam: a *Drogisterij* sells non-prescription drugs and toiletries and an *Apotheek* will make up prescriptions for you. If you need a prescription making up, the **Central Medical Service** (0900 503 2042) will advise you on what to do. Chemists (*apotheek*) are usually open Monday through to Saturday from 0830 to 1700. When closed, each chemist displays a notice of where the nearest late-opening one is situated. The 24-hour service **Afdeling Inlichtingen Apotheken** (694 8709) will lead you to your nearest dispensing chemist.

GLB information

GLB Switchboard 623 6565 **Open** Monday-Sunday, 1000-2200

AIDS Helpline 0800 022 2220 **Open** Monday-Friday, 1400-2200

GALA (Amsterdam's Gay and Lesbian Association)
(PO Box 15815, Amsterdam 1001NH) 616 1979

GG and GD (Groenburgwal 44) 662 4206
Sexually transmitted disease clinic. Offers free examination and treatment. Phone to book or be seen immediately **Open** Monday-Friday 0800-2230

COC Amsterdam Rozenstraat 14, 623 4079
Information and drop-in centre and meeting place of a number of gay groups. Pop in at any time to pick up maps and informative leaflets

HIV Plus Line 685 0055 **Open** Monday, Wednesday and Friday 1300-1600. Tuesday and Thursday 2000-2230

Most embassies and consulates are situated in The Hague, however, a few also have offices in Amsterdam. Listed are the key ones but if your country is not here just phone directory enquiries (0900 8008) and ask for the number of your country's embassy.

Consulates and embassies

Australia Carnegielaan 3, 2517 KH, Den Hague (070 310 8200)

Austria Weteringschans 106 (626 8033)

Belgium Drentestraat 11 (642 9763)

Canada Sophialaan 7, 2514 JP, Den Hague (070 311 1600)

Denmark De Ruyterkade 139 (623 4145)

France Vijselgracht 2 (624 8346)

Germany De Lairessestraat 172 (673 6245)

Republic of Ireland Dr Kuyperstraat 9, 2514 BA, Den Hague (070 363 0993)

Italy Herengracht 609 (624 0043)

New Zealand Carnegielaan 10, 2517 KH, Den Hague (070 346 9324)

United Kingdom Koningslaan 44 (676 4343)

United States Museumplein 19 (575 5309)

Disabled access

People with disabilities should inform airlines and accommodation outlets of their disabilities when making reservations or bookings. Time may be required to make suitable arrangements. Enquire also about the availability of ramps, door widths and other facilities. Amsterdam is not a wheelchair-friendly city – not because they don't care about the concerns of the disabled, they do, but because of the historical layout of the city, with its narrow streets and properties. For specific information geared towards disabled travellers to Amsterdam you should contact **Federatie Nederlandse Gehandicaptenraad**, Postbus 1693500, AD Utrech, the Netherlands (030 231 3454). Amsterdam also has special taxi services specifically for disabled persons. These require advance booking. Contact these companies direct, any weekday between 0900 and 1800 (613 4134, 633 3943 or 655 6729).

Getting in touch

Using the phone Most of the phone booths dotted around the city require pre-paid phonecards that can be purchased at train stations, tobacconists, post offices or tourist information offices. They are brightly coloured affairs, usually green, with a big KPN logo to identify them. Some phone kiosks in Centraal Station and at the airport accept euro coins; a minimum of €0.20 is required for a local call. Each phone kiosk will indicate the country codes of the most popular tourist home countries. To make an international call, dial 00 followed by your country code, then the national area code (usually leaving off an initial 0) and then the local number. International calls are cheaper during the hours between 2000 and 0800; and calls from Amsterdam to other European countries are not billed at the international rate. As with most countries, beware of making calls from your hotel; these will usually cost you a fortune. If you should need to use the phone then prior to calling you should nip down to reception and ask if they can supply you with a tariff.

Postal services Post offices are open Monday to Friday from 0900 to 1700. Some are also open on late-shopping nights (Thursday or Friday) and on Saturday from 1000 to 1300. There is even an all-night post office at **Nieuwezijds Voorburgwal**, behind the Royal Palace. At busy times there are counters labelled for certain functions only – remember to check before you queue. Posting a letter or postcard to anywhere in the EU costs €0.45; postcards to destinations outside Europe cost €0.55; letters up to 20g cost €0.75. Mail takes about three days to arrive in the UK, five to six days to arrive in North America and six to eight days to arrive in Australia and New Zealand. To post international letters or cards, remember to drop them into the *Overige* slot on the mail boxes. Post boxes are dotted all around the city. If you plan to change your address frequently, people can write to you at the following 'Poste Restante' address: **Poste Restante** Hoofdpostkantoor PTT, Singel 250, 1016 AB (556 3311). They are open Monday to Friday from 0830 to 1800 and Saturday from 0900 to 1200. They must make sure that your name is written clearly on the front of the envelope and the words 'Poste Restante' are written on the top left-hand side of the envelope. To collect your mail, go in person, to the main counter, and don't forget to take with you your passport or other photographic form of identification. The main city post offices are as follows: **Hoofdpostkantoor, Singel 250,** on the corner of

Radhuisstraat; **Oosterdokskade 5**, just east of Centraal Station; **St Antoniebreestraat 16**, near Niewmarkt; and **Waterlooplein 2**, in the Stadhuis.

Internet

Amsterdam embraced the internet-café culture many years ago and now it is hard to find a district without one. There are even internet terminals in its coffeeshops and bars. Charges obviously vary, but as a guide **EasyEverything** charges according to how busy the place is and it works out at around €2.50 for 45 to 60 minutes. Late in the evenings you can get about three hours for this price. An average price for all other cafés is around €3 per hour. There are also private internet booths similar to phone kiosks on many central plazas – all marked clearly with a big @. A normal phone card gives you access to the net and e-mail facilities. The most conveniently situated ones are at Centraal Station, on the Spui and near Max Euweplein. Try any of the following centrally located cafés: **Cyber Café** at Nieuwendyke 19; **EasyEverything** at Damrak 33 and Reguliersbreestraat 22 (both stay open for 24 hours); **Internet Café** at Korte Nieuwendijk 30; **Cybercorner** at Transvaalstraat 4; **Boek 'n Serve** at Ferdinand Bolstraat 151-153; **Maatschappij voor Oude** at Nieuwmarkt 4; **Café Tops** at Prinsengracht 480; **Kinko's, Inc.** at 62 Overtoom; and **The MAD Processor** at Bloemgracht 82.

Getting out

Calendar of events

Amsterdam stages various knees-ups and commemorations that lure in the tourists. **Koninginnedag** is a celebration of Queen Beatrix's birthday, or, more correctly, her mother's birthday. Beatrix was actually born in January but the weather in April is better suited to the street festivals and celebrations. You can toast Queenie in the company of queens if you like – head for the gay street parties on Reguliersdwarsstraat and around the Homomonument. Accommodation at this time of year is hard to find so make sure you book reasonably early. The Dutch get two public holidays in May. The 4 May sees the National Monument and the Homomonument become the focus for **Herdenkingsdag** (Remembrance Day) in honour of victims of the Second World War. The day after, on **Bevrijdingsdag** (Liberation Day), street parties are held around the two monuments. Towards the end of May or early June, over 5,000 people partake in the **Grachtenloop** (Canal run) and jog around all of Amsterdam's canals for charity. Bagsy a position at any of the main canals or see the runners sprinting off (or limping home) from the centre of this event, at the Stadsschouwburg. In June the **Festival of Holland** takes centre stage in the city. Part of the **Amsterdam Arts Adventure**, this is the city's equivalent of the Edinburgh Festival, and it lasts for the duration of the month. As the saying goes, 'there will be something for everyone', and complementing a full programme of events and activities, the streets colourfully ablaze with entertainers as well as people dressed up and standing still like statues, merely purporting to be entertainers. Hot on June's heels, and not to be confused with the Festival of Holland, the **Summer Festival** offers entertainments of a more avant-garde nature aimed to entertain and usually free of charge. The third Monday of August brings **Hartjesdag Zeedijk** (Hearts Day) where men and women of all persuasions 'drag' themselves up and the best, or most beautiful, is crowned before all. August also welcomes **De Parade**, which takes place in the Martin Luther King Park, beside the Amstel on the southern outskirts of town. Various theatre groups and individuals put on performances and cabarets of varying degrees of competency. Old showman-style masters of ceremony introduce you to the acts from stages set in front of makeshift auditoriums. Prices vary for each show and seats fill quickly. And, at the end of the month, there's **Uitmarkt**, a maze of happenings where all of the city's arty types and institutions preview the forthcoming delights of their season. Outdoor stages, and various cultural buildings in areas including Museumplein and the Dam, play host to all manner of performances.

Into Autumn, and September sees the **Bloemen Corso** (Flower Parade) on the first Saturday of the month, where a parade of floats bedecked in flowers motors slowly from Noordwijk through to Haarlem. September is also the time of the Jordaan Festival, a series of neighbourhood street parties that run right throughout the month, encouraging residents (and tourists!) to drink and be extremely merry, alfresco-style. The **Amsterdam Leather Fest** comes around in late October or early November. This ten-day event is one of the world's largest leather festivals and leathermen from all over the world converge on the city to show off their cowhide garb and accessories. Halfway through the month of November comes **Sinterklaas** – the Arrival of Santa Claus. In Amsterdam, Santa arrives, in seemingly prosaic fashion, hopping off a steamboat at Centraal Station and is given the keys to the city from the burgomaster on the Dam. He then parades around the city on a white horse with his assistant 'Black Pete' to the sheer delight of watching children. It is unclear as to why Santa is always accompanied by a black assistant – one popular explanation is that poor Black Pete has been down so many chimneys that he simply cannot get clean. Hmmm. And then, to finish the year in true Dutch style, there's the **Cannabis Cup**, the annual marijuana tasting festival sponsored by the spliff-fanatic's magazine of choice, *High Times*. About 2,000 judges sample and report on where they think the best plants in the city are sold and what they are. Coffeeshops give pride of place to their certificates and rosettes. And, no, I'm afraid I don't know how you apply to officiate.

Gay events

The world-famous **Amsterdam Gay Pride** comes around every year during the first weekend of August. The celebrations are co-ordinated by the **Gay Business Association**, founded in 1995 and now a force of over 80 gay-related companies. The main goal of the GBA and this annual event is to provide a series of parties and activities that will bring more liveliness to Amsterdam as a whole. This is the largest gay event in the whole of the Netherlands and, together with Queen's Day and the start of the cultural season, Uitmarkt, is one of the largest outdoor events of the year. Every first August weekend, several hundreds of thousands of people take to the streets with the party spirit coursing through their veins. If you're planning on heading over for the event be sure to book your accommodation early (many hotel rooms are booked a year in advance for this four-day event). Check out the website **www.amsterdampride.nl** regularly for up-to-date information. The highlight is the **Canal Parade**, when dressed-up boats and barges float down the Prinsengracht. The whole weekend, though, is littered with activities and you'll find the city's streets lined with the smiles and colours of a mixed international gay crowd. Leather fetishists should make their way over for the aforementioned Amsterdam Leather Fest, in late October.

April 30 Queen's Day
May 4 Memorial Day
May 5 Liberation Day
May Grachtenloop (late May/early June)
June Festival of Holland
July Summer Festival
August Amsterdam Gay Pride (first weekend in August)
August Hearts Day (third Monday in August)
August De Parade
October Amsterdam Leather Fest (late October/early November)
November Sinterklaas – the Arrival of Santa Claus
November 25-29 Cannabis Cup

Public holidays

The locals have several days off throughout the year, and they notably let their hair down on and in advance of two such occassions – the party atmosphere that accompanies the Queen's birthday celebrations and the wild all-night revelling that has become the norm come New Year's Eve.

January 1 New Year's Day
March/April Good Friday
March/April Easter Monday
April 30 Queen's Day
May 4 Remembrance Day
May 5 Liberation Day
May 9 Ascension Day
May Whit Sunday
May Whit Monday
December 25 Christmas Day
December 26 Boxing Day

Opening hours

The Amsterdam week gets off to a late start, with many shops and businesses not opening until noon. For the rest of the week, they tend to get going about 0900 and close about 1800. Many shops are now starting to stay open seven days a week. Some also stay open late on Thursday and Friday evenings. There are also night shops (*avondwinkels*), some of which stay open right around the clock. Museums, by and large, tend to be shut on Mondays and open Tuesday through to Saturday from around 1000 until 1700, and Sunday afternoons too. Listings magazines such as *Day and Night* should give you information on those venues with indeterminate hours.

Getting news

Newspapers

Holland's biggest-selling newspaper is right-wing *De Telegraaf*. Brits will be surprised to hear that it is the closest thing the Dutch have to a tabloid. The lefty-young at heart can pick up a copy of either *De Volkskrant* or *Het Parool*, or, for those that float somewhere around the centre, there's the *NRC Handelsblad*, a popular paper with a comprehensive coverage of the news and arts. Weekend papers are, mysteriously, something of a non-entity in Amsterdam. Still, Brits should be able to pick up their beefy weekenders and the *International Herald Tribune* should be available at some of the better-stocked newsagents, such as the shop at Centraal Station, where a comprehensive list of international publications can be found.

Gay press

Gay News Amsterdam is the biggest bilingual (Dutch and English), monthly gay publication there is. It has all the latest information on bar news, club nights and everything else that you need to know and is available free from all gay outlets or for €3.15 at many English-language bookshops and news-stands. The monthly, bilingual *Gay and Night* magazine is widely circulated throughout the Netherlands and Belgium and is available free from some gay venues. It too can be bought for €3.60 from many newsstands and bookshops. The *Amsterdam Gay Map* has all Amsterdam's gay venues marked, plus additional information, and is a valuable source for every gay tourist. This is available free from COC and many gay venues.

Television

Dutch television is nothing to write home about. You will, however, find English-language programmes. You're best off going one better, though, and finding the English-*produced* stuff – cable TV is big business in the Netherlands, and you should be able to find BBC1 and BBC2 there. MTV and CNN could be on the bandwidth too. If not, at least the choice of crap is far greater, with a multi-lingual pot-pourri of satellite programmes from all over the globe. **MVS TV** is a gay and lesbian scene and lifestyle cable channel that runs for a mere hour on Monday evenings.

Radio

If you've had all you can take of BBC World Service, you can flit between the popular choices of Radio Honderd for a wide and intellectual variety of youthful music from all over the world to the Dutch Classic FM station if you prefer to see in the evenings in a more serene fashion. **MVS Radio** is Amsterdam's only gay and lesbian station. It's non-commercial and broadcasts daily for three hours between 1800 and 2100. It aims to further tolerance and invigorate gay pride. Reports on the local scene and various programmes, most notably Alien – the anything-goes talk show where callers put across their (sometimes colourful) opinions.

Scene

2

You and the law

The spirit of tolerance and freedom within the Netherlands is refreshing. As ties between Europe become ever-more entwined, its ministers could do a lot worse than look upon Amsterdam as a shining example of how things should be: its liberal air is almost tangible. Following a framework of legislation put in place three years earlier, on 1 April 2001, Dutch gay and lesbian couples were legally allowed to be wed. As the clock struck midnight, Amsterdam City Hall bore witness to the city's first four gay marriages. Indeed, parity with heterosexuals extended to a full sweep of the matrimonial board, with homosexuals also having the right to divorce each other. Gay couples were also granted the right to adopt children. Needless to say, gay couples kissing or holding hands in public is no more shocking a sight to the Amsterdam local than one of his fellow citizens swearing at the pedestrian who transgresses into his bike lane. Still, whilst all this paints a rather rosy picture and suggests that Amsterdam has moved with the times, there are still inequalities. Lesbians, certainly, are hard done by. Their's is a much thinner slice of the scenic pie. There are only a handful of bars, clubs and club nights which cater for them, and very few of these are exclusive. As one local guide pointed out, you almost need a maths degree to make sure you turn up at the right place on the right night at the right time. All the same, lesbians flock to Amsterdam in their hordes. And why wouldn't they? More than anywhere in the world, this is a city where you can flaunt and enjoy your sexuality freely.

Age of consent

Homosexuality was legalised in the Netherlands way back in 1811 (it took Britain another 150-odd years to catch up). The age of consent for gay sex came down and then down again and is now on par with heterosexuals at 16. For prostitutes, however, the age has remained at 18 years.

Sexual activity

Cruising

Cruising is really the domain of countries where prohibition and inequality loom large. In the UK, for example, there is no legalised sex industry. Brothels are illegal, hiding behind the façade of 'Massage Parlours'. Red-light districts have bulbs that glow dimly, with police and residents working together to free their neighbourhoods of filfth, terrified that crime and indecency are about to bud on their doorsteps. These attitudes mirror the legal inequalities of the UK. In Amsterdam, though cruising exists, it is not an integral part of the recognised scene, as it is in, say, London. It doesn't need to be. You can make the acquaintance of rent boys within minutes of your arrival into the city. You can openly parade your sexuality without fear of offending anyone.

Which all sounds like a bit of a death knell for cruising then. Well, not exactly; it does still go on and is still generally tolerated in Amsterdam, although only in places where it's not likely to cause offence. Discreet sex in such places is acceptable. In the past, some such areas were designated 'tolerance zones'. Cities like London looked to the Dutch example, saw its relative success, and tried – and failed – to implement such a scheme for the notorious Russell Square. In Amsterdam, quite a few of the places that were first appropriated for this purpose, such as the Nieuwe Meer in the south-west of the city, have now been redeveloped to make them more open and less desirable for frisky gay men.

It's highly unlikely that you'll be arrested for cruising in Amsterdam. Such is the city's relaxed air that even its police officers have been known to walk into cottages with their radios cranked up to full volume from a hundred yards away. They are unlikely to try and catch you in the act. They will be more concerned with moving you on. In short, though you've no real need to cruise, you can and you will find like-minded others there when you do. If you do go cruising, be discreet and sensible and take the time to get acquainted with how and where the land lies.

Drugs

There's a broad smile on my face as I type. The freely available sale and use of cannabis in the Netherlands is just one of the wonderful things about the city. It's one of the main reasons that the tourist trade has blossomed. I'm sure that statement will have the Dutch Tourist Authority pulling their hair out – their city is beautiful, weighed down in history and culture; its people, its landscape, they are the draw for the tourists.... Maybe – indeed, the last six years have seen 400-plus coffeeshops reduce to just over 300 in number, suggesting an industry slightly on the wane – but make no mistake, Amsterdam's liberal yet controlled stance on drugs is one hell of a plus point on the city's curriculum vitae.

Dos and don'ts

Like any other international city, ecstasy, speed and cocaine are easily available but are still illegal, although possession of such (if the amount is small and obviously for personal use) will usually get you a telling-off and see to the drug being confiscated. If you are after a harder drug – ecstasy or cocaine, for example – do not buy it off the street. More often than not you'll be landed with caffeine, bicarbonate or some other worthless substance produced solely to con the visitor. Your best bet is to ask around at gay bars and clubs, who can usually be trusted for their information. Alternatively, visit any one of a number of 'smart shops' which sell a variety of chemical substances that are not (yet) illegal. Be straight with the proprietor and ask for a substitute for cocaine or the drug of your choice and you will be surprised at the service (and choice) that you will get.

The sale and use of cannabis in the Netherlands is, technically, still illegal. However, you are allowed to purchase it in quantities not in excess of five grams, and this amount you are also allowed to carry upon your person. That is the underlying (albeit brief) basis of the law. Though the law may seem liberal, there are many establishments, certain bars and clubs for example, where the consumption of cannabis is frowned upon, so don't assume you've been given a green light to smoke anywhere you please. Look around: if anyone else is smoking, then you may be free to do the same. If you are unsure it is always better to ask.

Coffeeshops

Ah yes, that rather nice euphemism for drugs' den! Coffee bean afficionados make no mistake: this is the domain of the smoker. There is a separate counter that sells the weed, usually located at the back of the place, where a well-thumbed menu of hash (resin) or grass (buds) is on view. In some coffeeshops, particularly where they are also licensed to sell alcohol, the hash counter may be on a different level to the bar. By asking to see 'the menu' staff will know exactly what you are after and direct you to the appropriate place. To the uninitiated, reading the menu is akin to deciphering a foreign language. The sight of your jaw hitting the counter is usually an indication to the vendor that either you (a) don't know what you are looking at, or (b) do, and assume yourself landed in heaven! If it's the former, then be sure to ask the vendor for his or her recommendation. They will respect you for this and will be more inclined to help you in your selection, although don't expect too much attention in the tourist-trap shops. Explain your tolerance level and suggest that you would like to start off on something mild (or strong). Don't be an arsehole and bait for ridicule by asking if it is 'good stuff' – it most certainly will be, and trying the Dutch home-grown varieties will soon make you realise how poor the 'good stuff' you smoke at home actually is.

Those who do not usually smoke may be able to find 'space cakes' (chocolate brownies laced with cannabis) on sale in one of the shops, but these are becoming harder and harder to find. The time it takes to get into your system (up to two hours, and even longer if you have just had a meal) gave the Dutch government cause for concern, as an increasing number of tourists were consuming more than was good for them. They 'asked' for space cakes to be made unavailable. Nevertheless, some outlets do still sell them. If you are going to indulge, be aware of their latent effects. One space cake is equivalent to one joint, so leave it at least an hour before you decide to go for another. The effect of space cakes is more intense than smoking equivalent cannabis, and their effects can range from subtle to strong.

Most coffeeshops also sell ready-rolled joints. This is the most expensive way of smoking but it does save the novice the embarrassment of rolling his or her own. You are allowed to roll and smoke your own dope in any coffeeshop, although it is common courtesy to purchase something, such as a toastie and a drink, before you make use of their sofas and tables. In any event you'll need something to satisfy an imminent bout of the munchies!

Limits and prices

More often than not, cannabis will come in weights of one to five grams, which is the maximum legal limit per transaction. Purchasing smaller amounts is a good opportunity for you to try out different strains and different coffeeshops. Pricewise, it depends on where you are. As a general rule of thumb, the more touristy the area the more you will pay and the poorer the standard of service will be. The downside of this rule is that the coffeeshops are less atmospheric the further away you go from the tourist areas. Expect to pay about €4 per gram-baggie of a fairly decent bud – ridiculously cheap for residents of countries where dope can only be purchased illegaly. The five-gram-baggies will cost in the region of €12. As a tourist, you won't be able to take any of your purchase home with you (sniffer dogs at airport terminals will take a leg off you) so don't buy more than you can feasibly get through during your time in the city.

Cannabis cannot be served to anyone under 18 years of age and the maximum amount that you can buy at any one shop is five grams per day (which should be more than enough for even the most hardened smoker). Most coffeeshops will provide complimentary rolling papers and cardboard strips for the filters. Many will have bongs and pipes for use (although most will be clogged and in need of a clean). A small deposit will be required for these. Bear in mind that few coffeeshops are licensed to serve alcohol *as well as* cannabis. Probably a blessing, since you don't really want to be mixing the two at the same time. Not all coffeeshops are immediately recognisable: on the window there should be a sticker with green and white diagonals and 'Coffee Shop' pronounced in bold, black letters. Coffeeshops are legally obliged to ensure that none of its patrons cause excessive noise or make a nuisance of themselves to the general public. If you are guilty of such affray, you may well be asked to leave.

Alcohol

Beer is the Dutch tipple, and nationals can choose between three internationally-renowned brews – Heineken, Grolsch and Amstel – which you'll find to be far more intense and flavoursome than the exported versions you might have tasted back home. The traditional Dutch foamy head on a glass of lager is not there to con you out of a few fingers of beer. It is there because the beer is pumped through under high pressure. If you think that you've received only half a glass and dare to ask the person behind the bar to 'fill it up to the top, please' then take the time to stop and stare as a deathly quiet descends throughout the room and heads turn silently towards you, in the manner of those old Western movies where strange gunslingers sashayed through the bar doors for the first time. Like poor, old Oliver, you're unlikely to get more: that's how a glass of beer is pulled so you'd better get used to it! You have to be over 16 years of age to order alcoholic drinks, but over 18 years of age to order spirits and drinks in excess of 15-per-cent volume.

Bars and clubs

Bar culture is a big part of city life, and for those that prefer supping to toking, there's a good variety of places to drink yourself to inebriation. Bars largely fall into two categories: the brown café, where brown denotes the tobacco-stained colour and lived-in feel of the place; and the more upmarket, designer bars, which gear towards the young and slick.

For the gay night owl there is a more than adequate gay scene, although, for a city the size of Amsterdam, there does seem to be a shortage of regular gay club nights, particularly those for the hard-house, trance and garage scene. Club iT does its best although it is only pink on a Saturday night and there's a feeling of 'we should be so grateful for letting us in' that somewhat takes the edge off what should be a pleasant experience. In contrast, there is an abundance of bars and clubs for the gay male with a penchant for leather and sex. Fine, if you like that sort of thing, but there are frustratingly few venues for the younger gay male who wants the sex and harder edged music without having to, or wanting to, dress up in leather and latex.

Some bars open their doors in the morning from around 1000. Others open at around 1700 and generally stay open until 0100 during the week and as late as 0300 at weekends. Clubs start opening their doors from about 2100 onwards and stay open as late as 0500 the following morning.

Darkrooms

The term is descriptive enough. Darkrooms (or sometimes playrooms) are places, usually at the back of bars, clubs and saunas, with very little or no lighting at all where men go to have sex. If you're new to the darkroom phenomenon, then you might be a little timid about entering into these spaces. Quite why, in a city with such liberal attitudes towards sex between men, darkrooms are necessary is something of a mystery. They are, of course, all a bit of a thrill, but you should be aware that they can also be risky. Some of these rooms verge on pitch-black. Subdued lighting would better facilitate the practice of safe sex (although proprietors are forced to supply condoms and safe-sex information). Also, if you're fussy about who pokes around your nether regions then you really might not be able to tell how great- or gross-looking the man accommodating you is. Still, the types that tend to use these rooms either find the darkness a turn-on, or an ice-breaker that makes them less self-conscious. Darkrooms can be found in dozens of venues throughout Amsterdam. If you're going to use them think carefully about safe sex and make sure money and valuables aren't in danger of being fondled out of your pockets.

Accommodation

Gay accommodation in Amsterdam, is very nearly always full to capacity, particularly between April and September, so try and book your rooms as far in advance as you can. For some gays and lesbians, staying in exclusively gay accommodation is all part of the experience. However, Amsterdam hotel and guest-house proprietors are so relaxed in their attitudes that staying in non-gay accommodation should not really be any cause for concern. I recommend that you find out the areas you wish to concentrate your stay in and then find convenient accommodation (gay or non-gay) that will best serve you as a base. It is worth noting that it is illegal in the Netherlands for accommodation proprietors to turn away same-sex couples. In the city there is a raft of budget accommodation – most of the rooms in this category will be clean and comfortable but the standard of room furnishings and facilities will be bordering on the basic. In short, like everything else in life, you get what you pay for! The majority of the listings in this guide are either designated gay-owned or -run or are gay-friendly and close to, or within, the gay areas of the city.

Saunas

In a city as small as Amsterdam, you're never going to be too spoilt for choice when it comes to choosing where to steam your bits. The city has three saunas and a gymnasium with a small sauna unit. The three saunas are of a very high quality and a visit to any of them shouldn't disappoint. As I've written before, if you have never been to a gay sauna before then there is only one piece of advice I can give you – go now. Don't think about the stereotyped characters you've heard about frequenting these places. Times have moved on and you'll find a variety of types and ages. You don't have to consent to anything you don't want to and you will generally find the facilities clean and welcoming and the staff helpful and accommodating. Just go and enjoy yourself!

Prostitution

The majority of Amsterdam's prostitutes belong to a union called The Red Thread. This membership offers them considerable rights and entitlements to respect and behaviour. You should not take photographs of the women working behind the neon-lit windows of the red-light district. Deviation from this very simple rule will get you a swift visit from a big, burly man who will demand that you explain yourself. The prostitutes behind the windows also have access to an emergency button that, once pressed, will automatically emit an ear-piercing siren and summon the police who will undoubtedly side with the girl. If you want a photo, ask the girl how much she will charge for the privilege.

Rent boys are also subject to a certain number of rules and regulations, particularly the ones in the so-called 'Houses of Boys'. Negotiations on price and the service you can expect to receive should be discussed and made clear prior to any act of indulgence. You should treat the boys with dignity and respect, and vice versa. Don't expect love or counselling for any problems you might have – though they may offer a sympathetic ear, you are merely one in a long line of 'transactions'. They offer a service, you pay for the service and that's as far as any relationship goes!

Using this guide

Regarding the listings that fall within 'The guide' section of this book, I have tried to convey as much information in the most basic way possible. No unnecessary symbols, nothing unjustly partisan – just facts and honest opinion. These listings are thorough and up-to-date. You can substantiate this for yourself. If you have any further information or corrections – or any free tickets or membership passes(!) – please contact me at **gaytimes@absolutepress.demon.co.uk**. In the section, 'A few things', I have tried to offer you a manageable choice of some of the best non-gay-specific attractions that the city has to offer, from its rich seam of cultural and historical attractions. For those that feel nauseous at the thought of ploughing through a separate city guide, I hope that I have sketched out enough ideas to keep you busy. For those seeking a more thorough introduction, I would recommend comprehensive Amsterdam guide books such as *Rough Guide* or *Time Out*.

Proprietors' note

A note to venue proprietors: help me out! Some of you are notoriously difficult to get information out of! If your venue or establishment has not been included or lacks relevant information, then please contact me in order that any amendments can be made for subsequent editions.

Newcomers

If you're new to the country or have never been to a gay venue before and are wary about going in on your own, contact the gay switchboard to find out the best way of starting out on the Amsterdam scene. There are loads of others out there in the same position. You've nothing to fear. Age has never been an issue in gay establishments – young and old mix extremely well in most venues. If you think you're 'past that sort of thing' then think again – you are missing out on an awful lot.

Definitions

For the listings that lie within **The guide** section of this book the following definitions apply: I have listed the standard opening hours of establishments under the **Open** fields. This field follows the description for each listed venue/night. These hours are forever at the mercy of promoters changing their minds, late licenses being sought or cancelled, and you should always check prior to any specific visit, that the night and/or venue you are travelling to is (a) running; and (b) running to the same hours as listed. The gay scene is probably the fastest shifting scene there is: things change! I have also indicated the **Price** range you can expect to pay (assume 'free' when not included). The accommodation listings retain the price field, which, unless otherwise stated, relates to the price you can expect to pay as a couple sharing a double/twin room (with en-suite facilities, if available), booking in high season. These usually constitute the most expensive rooms available. In most cases there are standard rooms available at a lower cost and some establishments will offer a reduced rate for mid-week stays. Ask! Where any of these fields are missing you can assume that they are not relevant or that the information was impossible to extract!

It is always worth mentioning this travel guide as the source for your enquiry. Some establishments expressed an interest in offering a reduction to readers of this guide. Details of accommodation have been provided by the guest-house or hotel proprietors themselves. The accommodation listings are limited to establishments that are gay-run, gay-owned or exclusively gay or gay-friendly venues that lie within the heart of the gay areas. As before, I request that you e-mail me with your additions, retractions and amendments: **gaytimes@absolutepress.demon.co.uk**.

Disclaimer

The publishers, contributors and myself cannot be held responsible for any action whatsoever brought against you or any acquaintance of yours, nor can we be held responsible for any incident caused to you or any acquaintance of yours from any use of the listings.

A few things

3

A few museums

Some of Amsterdam's most famous museums underwent change and renovation at the turn of the century, including three of its most famous spaces: the Van Gogh Museum, Anne Frankhuis and Rembrandthuis. So too Museumplein, the great stretch of lawn with four of the city's finest cultural centres as its anchor points. Though a relatively small city, Amsterdam has a variety of museums that are bound to please and the city's recent investment in these places is a sign of their popularity and cultural and historical significance. These are some of the best.

Rijksmuseum

Stadhouderskade 42 Phone **674 7047**
What started off as a collection of 200 paintings confiscated from the exiled Prince William V in 1798, has become the Netherlands' largest and most impressive collection of painting and sculpture. Completed in 1885, the building was designed as a great entrance to the city, which at the time was surrounded by fields and marshland. Today, the building holds over 5,000 paintings, 30,000 sculptures, 17,000 historical objects and over 1,000,000 prints and drawings, which span from the fifteenth century to the mid-twentieth. Probably the most famous art work on show is Rembrandt's *Night Watch*, which sits amongst the Dutch Masters' section in the Gallery of Honour on the top floor, which also features stunning paintings by Vermeer, Frans Hals, Jan Steen and other notable Dutch artists. In less-busy rooms you can see centuries-old dolls' houses and furniture. The museum has two different entrances which stand on opposite sides of the grand underpass that cuts right through the centre of the building. The Rijksmuseum is a must-see national treasure. **Open** Monday-Sunday 1000-1700 **Price** €8.50 (free for under-19s)

Stedelijk Museum

Paulus Potterstraat 13 Phone **573 2911**
This is the national museum for modern and contemporary art. After massive investment, work is due to begin on two new wings by the end of 2002, as well as renovations to the main building. In view of any subsequent spell of closure you'd be well advised to brave the queues and visit one of Amsterdam's most stunning collections of art whilst you still can. The changing face of the permanent collection housed on the top floor includes great works by modernist luminaries such as Cézanne, Matisse, Picasso, Chagall and Kandinsky to name but a few, through to the post-war works of Rothko, Kelly, Newman, Lichtenstein, Judd and Warhol. Temporary exhibitions roll through the ground-floor rooms and reflect new painting, sculpture and photography and 'new media' work renowned for sparking 'is it art?' type questions (controversial London artist Tracey Emin is scheduled to show in September 2002). There are also large retrospectives featuring other well-known artists, and small shows presenting younger artists. If you're thirsty or peckish then you can head for the Appel-bar and restaurant, so vibrantly ameliorated by CoBrA artist Karel Appel. **Open** Monday-Sunday 1100-1700 **Price** €5

The Van Gogh Museum

Paulus Potterstraat 7 Phone **570 5200**
The Van Gogh Museum is the biggest money-spinning tourist attraction in Amsterdam, attracting the sort of queues that up-and-coming artists can only dream about. Ironic then that this is an artist who sold only two paintings in his lifetime! The museum houses over 200 Van Gogh paintings (the largest collection in the world), over 500 sketches and several examples of his Japanese prints. Further to this, you can view a collection of works by his contemporaries; letters from the artist to his family and friends; a complete press archive and a collection of prosthetic ears that the artist experimented with in later life. (Just joking on that last one.) The museum owns the priceless copyright on the lot! There is no sure-fire way of beating the queues, but the early morning game plan seems to be the one that most people go for: follow suit and you could find yourself in a huge bottleneck as the first few in the queue studiously pore over every word on every descriptive panel. It is wiser to go during lunch when the queues subside just a little. Either way, it's well worth the effort to see the riches of possibly the most popular modern artist of them all. **Open** Monday-Sunday 1000-1800 **Price** €7

Hash, Marijuana and Hemp Museum

Oudezijds Achterburgwal 138 Phone **623 5961**
Located, quite ironically, in an old tobacco warehouse, this small museum-cum-shrine to the original pot plant keeps on going despite a great critical divide as to its worthiness. Much like Marmite – you either love it or you hate it. Either way, it is shortly due to increase in size, expanding into the former premises of the Tattoo Museum (still listed in some guidebooks despite closing down in 2000) and plans are being discussed to introduce and show more historical implements and artefacts (if those are the correct terms) of cannabis culture. Presently, the museum shows, among loads of other things, the complete gro-cycle of many strains of plant, leading to the shrine of many a pot smoker's dream – the gro-room, packed with budding plants the likes of which most pot buffs will never see again. Well, not in their conscious moments at least. **Open** Monday-Sunday 1100-2200 **Price** €5.75

Amsterdam Erotic Museum

Oudezijds Achterburgwal 54 Phone **624 7303**
When you get museum overload it's nice just to wander round a building such as this and just be, well... entertained. There are interesting bits (such as devices that can offer discreet sexual stimulation) and there are fun bits (such as being able to have your photo taken in a mock-up of a prozzie's red-light district window – mother went mad!). All in all, it's amusing rather than educational, and with five floors to explore, it should keep you busy for, erm, 35 minutes or so. **Open** Sunday-Thursday 1100 -0100. Friday-Saturday 1100-0200 **Price** €2.75

Madame Tussauds

Dam Square Phone **523 0623**
Recently redesigned and renovated with the addition of a new floor, Madame Tussauds will no doubt continue to try and dupe – sorry, I meant to say enthral – visitors to her collection of plus-five-foot recycled candles. I'm cynical towards the concept behind Madame T's. I'm sure that in bygone eras, collections such as these would have roused the pub-

lic interest. But today? No way. It's archaic and serves only to inflate the egos of those it caricatures (most of whom must recoil in utter embarrassment at the sight of themselves a few months on). Celebrity faces are ubiquitous across our media these days: why on earth would anyone want to queue to pay to see quasi-likenesses? 'Celebrity Cocks of The Rich and Famous', on the other hand, now that would be worth the admission fee! Anyway, rant over with, Tussauds is still a big tourist draw. **Open** Monday-Sunday 1000-1830 (except through July 15-August 31 when hours run 0930-2030) **Price** €12.50

Sex Museum

Damrak 18 Phone 622 8376
Sigh... is this really the best they can come up with? More amusing than arousing: a plethora of devices, artefacts, pictures, antique implements and models. Topics covered throughout the museum are bestiality, sadomasochism, watersports, fisting, huge dongs and dong holes... and that's just the octogenarian quarter (hee-hee). Some of the erotic artwork, cartoons and sculpture aside, you're more likely to be titilated by the accoutrements in any one of the city's sex shops than you are with those on display here. There's a chance that the straights might wince at the odd S&M item, but, in all honesty, the showroom of RoB holds more excitement than what's on offer here. Still, worth the couple of euros as this is a must-see bit of the Dam, if only for the quirkyness of it all. **Open** Monday-Sunday 1000-2330 **Price** €2.50

newMetropolis (NEMO)

Oosterdok 2 Phone **0900 - 9191100 (premium rate)**
Set in the harbour, between Centraal Station and the Maritime Museum, is the new Metropolis Science and Technology Centre, looking like the huge, green hull of a ship emerging out of the water. Virtual reality displays are the high point of this cutting-edge complex, inaugurated in 1997 and designed by Renzo Piano (one of the architectural duo responisble for Paris's Pompidou Centre). The view of the city from the rooftop café alone is worth the visit. NEMO takes in four levels of interactive learning – Why The World Works; Chain Reaction; Wonder Lab and Super Banker – where everything from making electricity to peering down microscopes is within your remit. **Open** Tuesday to Sunday 1000-1700 **Price** €8.50

Amsterdam Historisch Museum

Kalverstraat 92 Phone **5231743**
Halfway up Kalverstraat is one of the three entrances (you can also access from Nieuwezijds Voorburgwal and Sint Luciensteeg) to one of Amsterdam's must-definitely-see attractions. The Historical Museum of Amsterdam provides you with a compact and accessible introduction to the history of this fine city. The contents are arranged chronologically, from Amsterdam's foundation up to the twentieth century and for those of us who neglected to opt for Dutch as a second language (that's everyone then...) you can arm yourself with a file of explanations in English, obtained for free from the ticket desk. On the ground floor is a fascinating automatic map that lights up the sections of the city as it has grown over the years. Once the twentieth century has been reached, all the lights go out and it starts again. Loads of button-pushing and lever-throwing

exhibits that make the paintings and artefacts come to life (not literally, but bear with me). A whole room is dedicated to the Miracle of Amsterdam (see the Sint Nicolaaskerk entry in 'A Few Churches') which believers find fascinating and atheists (ahem) even more so. Make your way up the spiral staircase and you'll find another fun room where you can listen to the famous carillons of the city and even have a go yourself by trying to recreate the one from the medieval Munttoren (Munt Plein). The watchful eye of the attendant will ensure you don't transgress into 'Ding, Dong Merrily on High'. Such fun! **Open** Monday-Friday 1000-1700. Saturday-Sunday 1100-1700 **Price** €6

Brilmuseum

Gasthuismolensteeg 7 Phone **421 2414**
I must have misheard my friend; I thought he said 'testicles', but no, this is the National Spectacles Museum, a personal collection of spectacles from around the world that spans four generations of opticians. My intial disappointment set aside, I trotted around this quirky and interesting attraction, which should appeal to anyone with a compelling propensity for face furniture. The four-storey house is jam-packed with pairs of glasses from nearly every country and period, including those bequeathed from celebrities past and present – Schubert, Buddy Holly and Dame Edna to name but a few. On the ground floor there is a spectacles shop in a re-created 1930s setting where you can find outlandish, dicreet and everything-in-between pairs of frames for a reasonable price. **Open** Wednesday-Friday 1200-1730. Saturday 1200-1700

Rembrandthuis

Jodenbreestraat 4-6 Phone **520 0400**
Rembrandt van Rijn lived and worked in this house from 1639 until 1658. In 1658, the artist was evicted by tax hounds. Perfectly ironic since today it ranks as one of the city's biggest earners. The artist lived here for nearly 20 years and his old house has been converted into a museum, one though that has been carefully restored to its original state using plans and descriptions that date back to the seventeenth century to ensure authenticity. The adjoining modern wing displays an impressive collection of more than 250 of his etchings, including a series of amusing self-portraits. Rembrandt immortalised himself in paint more than any other seventeenth-century artist: copious self-portraits and 'cameos' in many a crowd scene on some of his larger canvases. In the basement of the museum there is a slide show which starts flipping hourly, on the hour, until 1500 where you can learn about his life. You can also visit the house where he lived out the remainder of his life, at Rozengracht 184 in the Jordaan. **Open** Monday-Saturday 1000 - 1700. Sunday 1300-1700 **Price** €7

Joods Historisch Museum

Jonas Daniël Meijerplein Phone **626 9945**
This museum is a complex of four old Ashkenazi synagogues, displaying art, memorabilia and artefacts with the aim of exploring the history and identity of Dutch Jews over a span of 400 years. The glass and steel structure that provides the links to each of the seventeenth- and eighteenth-century main exhibition spaces echoes the museum's hope to provide a link from the past to the future for Jews and non-Jews alike. The New Synagogue area explains aspects of tradition, Zionism and the reaction

to persecution. The Great Synagogue is given over to the expositions of Judaism itself – the rituals, the festivals and the rites of passage. The Permanent Collection includes old clothing, photographs, religious artefacts, texts and artwork. Genuinely moving and thought-provoking and well worth a visit. **Open** Monday-Sunday 1100-1700 **Price** €5

Verzetsmuseum **Plantage Doklaan 61** Phone **620 2535**
Get a good insight into the 1940s Resistance movement as you study the newspaper clippings, photographs, makeshift secret equipment and tape recordings. The museum gives you a true sense of the plight of the ordinary citizens during Nazi occupation. Interactive exhibits inspire admiration as they illustrate the workings of the movement in the attempt to keep over a quarter of a million people in hiding. Fascinating stuff. **Open** Tuesday-Friday 1000-1700. Saturday-Monday 1300-1700 **Price** €4

Willet-Holthuysen Museum **Herengracht 605** Phone **523 1822**
Located at the southern end of the Herengracht, near Rembrandtplein, is the Willet-Holthuysen Museum, delightfully set in a seventeenth century canal house. For nearly two centuries it was occupied by a succession of the rich and famous of Amsterdam. The last incumbent was Sandrina Holthuysen, who spent most of her life married to Abraham Willet, an avid collector of glass, ceramics, silver, paintings and art books. Sandrina died alone in 1895, riddled with cancer and surrounded by her cats. She left the home and its contents as a museum to the city. Officials then filled the house with rich pickings from other bequests. Most of the rooms are now reconstructed as eighteenth-century period pieces, with the different collections scattered about the property, mainly museum-like in rather stiff salons and boudoirs. Apart from the formality of it all, this place will give you a good insider's view of what one of the statelier canal houses looked like. **Open** Monday-Friday 1000-1700. Saturday-Sunday 1100-1700 **Price** €4

Kattenkabinet **Herengracht 497** Phone **626 5378**
Deemed to be the only museum in the world devoted solely to cat-related works of art, this is the strange but enchanting collection put together by financier Bob Meijer whose own puss-puss, John Pierpont Morgan, died in 1984. The story goes that JPM received a special present from his master every five years; a portrait of himself to begin with, and then, five years later, his likeness cast in bronze. Others followed: a book of limericks and moggy-caricature-adapted dollar bills among them. Meijer obviously had no stomach for taxidermy – so you needn't fear bumping into the stiffened tomcat himself – but the extensive collection of paintings, sketches, drawings and objet d'art includes works by Picasso, Kipling and a host of other famous artists all lovingly assembled in commemoration of one man's feline friend. **Open** Monday-Friday 1000-0200. Saturday-Sunday 1300-1700 **Price** €4.75

Bijbels Museum **Herengracht 366** Phone **624 2436**
The Amsterdam Biblical Museum is situated in two canal houses that date back to 1662. The houses were built by Philips Vingboons, a

famous Dutch architect, by order of the Amsterdam merchant Jacob Cromhout. The ceiling in the main hall is painted with mythological images by Jacob de Wit, a noted Dutch painter. The museum was founded by Reverend Leendert Schouten who put his own collection on public display in 1851 and it is this collection that forms the heart of the museum, which is, namely, the Good Book itself. Among the other Bibles on display are the first Bible to be printed in the Low Countries, which dates back to 1477 and the *statenvertaling* from 1637, the first edition of the authorised Dutch translation. **Open** Monday-Saturday 1000-1700. Sunday 1300-1700 **Price** €3.65

Anne Frankhuis **Prinsengracht 263** Phone **556 7100**

It's incredible to think that probably our most vivid record of German occupation and the Holocaust was written by a teenage girl. Born in Frankfurt, Anne Frank's family fled to the Netherlands in 1933, when she was just four years old. She reached the age of eleven without a care, in the relatively safe confines of the Grachtengordel area of Amsterdam. When the Germans occupied the Netherlands in 1940, the protective bubble that Anne and her family had existed in was about to burst. Increasingly restricted by the anti-Jewish decrees and terrified by the deportations to the 'work camps' that began in 1942, the family went into hiding, into the annexe of the building that housed her father Otto's business. Anne begins writing her diary and continues over the course of the next two years whilst hiding in the claustrophobic space of the annexe. In 1944, these refugees are discovered and arrested and deported via the transit camp Westerbork. Whilst most of the occupants were sent to Auschwitz, Anne and her sister were sent to the Bergen-Belsen concentration camp, where they died within a short time of each other, Anne in March 1945, just one week before the German surrender. Otto was the only one of the annexe occupants to survive his ordeal, and on his return from Auschwitz he was handed the diary that had remained behind in Prinsengracht. He gave permission for it to be published and the book first appeared in 1947. Ten years later, the Anne Frank Foundation opened the house to a worldwide public. You can expect to join a long queue, no matter what time you get here, but a visit here is essential. **Open** 0900-2100 (reduced opening until 1900 from September to March) **Price** €6.50

Pianola Museum **Westerstraat 106** Phone **627 9624**

Have a guess what this place is full of? You're right – pianolas, loads of them, as well as some piano-playing machines thrown in for good measure. With a store of more than 14,000 rolls of perforated music to boot, there's no shortage of tunes. These were the jukeboxes of their day, and so if you fancy a knees-up to a bit of Gershwin or a hands-in-the-air moment to Debussy, then this could well be the place for you. **Open** Sunday 1300-1700 **Price** €3.50

Heineken Brouwerij **Stadhouderskade 78** Phone **523 9666**

Established here in 1867 this is the birthplace of Heineken beer. Brewery production ceased a few years ago in 1988 when the Heineken brewery in

Zoeterwoude took over production from the Amsterdam brewery. The Amsterdam site was then used as a reception centre for ten years. It became home to the 'Heineken Experience' in May 2001. This is a fun museum with loads of hi-tech info terminals, including a virtual experience ride where you are shrunk down to the size of a bottle size (yeah, you're going to need to use your imagination) and then taken on a journey around the bottling plant. At the end of the tour, which should last just over an hour, comes the highlight – a few free glasses of beer (it used to be 'all you can drink', but no longer – maybe they anticipated my visit?) and a gift (usually a Heineken glass). Well worth the few euros admission. **Open** Tuesday-Sunday 1000-1800 **Price** €5

A few churches

Of all the buildings in Amsterdam it is perhaps the churches that are at its architectural core, and that tell so much of the city's wonderful history. Indeed, the city's oldest building is the Old Church (originally the Church of St Nicholas), which dates back to around 1300. Further places of worship soon began to appear throughout the city. These medieval churches were Roman Catholic, and were all named after saints. After the Reformation, however, Protestants changed the names of these churches (to reflect the locations that the churches were in) and radically altered their interiors. Such was the turmoil, that all other religions bar Judaism were forced underground. Legislation though, was charecteristically laid-back, and ordinary houses were transformed into places of behind-closed-doors worship (witness one of the few remaining examples at Oudezijds Voorburgwal 40). The first Protestant churches appeared and were as stunning as their Catholic-commissioned ancestors. By the end of the eighteenth century though, religious equality was restored, and over the decades that followed, the first new Catholic churches began to appear.

Oude Kerk

Ouderkerksplein 23
Located in the heart of the red-light district and providing sanctuary for the guilty straight men who minutes before can be seen posturing and screaming to the girls in the windows 'You like that, doncha?' Most of this building dates back a number of centuries – the oldest part being the tower, which goes right back to 1300. The majority of the rest of the building is sixteenth century and many of the side chapels and transepts were added later. Some of the most interesting parts of the church are the tomb of Saskia van Uylenburgh (Rembrandt's first wife), and the magnificent painted, wooden vaults, which create a unique atmosphere and give away something of the building's unique history. There is also the secret door, five metres above ground and previously covered by plaster (in St Sebastiaanskapel, which leads through to the Ljzeren Kapel or Iron Chapel) which was a hiding place for important city documents until 1892. **Open** April-November: Monday-Saturday 1100-1700. Sunday 1300-1500. December-March: Sunday-Friday 1300-1500. Saturday 1100-1500 **Price** €3.75

Nieuwe Kerk

Dam Square Phone **626 8168**
In the late fourteenth century Amsterdam expanded rapidly. The church became a crowded place, and demand called for a second church. A wealthy merchant banker, Willem Eggert, donated his orchard and a large sum of money for construction works. It is after him that the Eggertkapel and the Eggertzaal are named. Before the turn of the century, construction was well under way, even though the Bishop only gave his approval in 1408. The outside was ornate, and so too was the rich Catholic interior, but the latter did not hold long. When Amsterdam took the side of the Protestants in 1578, the first protestant clergyman took to the pulpit. Consequently, the interior, or the Alteration as it was known, underwent radical changes. The statues and altarpieces were removed or destroyed and the walls were painted white. No less than three times, the church fell prey to heavy fires. In the winter of 1645, it was hit hardest. Plumbers left a burning pot unattended, the roof caught fire and disappeared completely in the blaze. The transept organ is one of the very few remaining items that survived. After the heaviest of these fires, the church was restored and further adorned. A new pulpit, a monumental organ and a brass choir screen were installed – all exquisite works of art in their own right. Over successive years, several additions followed, such as the stained-glass windows and the Remembrance window. Shortly before the inauguration of Queen Beatrix in 1980, the church re-opened its doors. Attendance at church services had dropped considerably, so it needed a new raison d'être. A foundation – De Nationale Stichting De Nieuwe Kerk – was established, and now the premises have become famous for exhibitions of treasures from faraway countries, showcasing familiar and less familiar cultures and religions. There is no charge to visit the church outside of its exhibition periods.
Open Monday-Sunday 1000-1800 **Price** Free, except for varying prices of exhibitions

Sint Nicolaaskerk

Prins Hendrikkade
Each late March the Roman Catholic community winds up their Silent Procession (Stille Omgang) at this restored nineteenth-century neo-Renaissance church, to commemorate the Miracle of Amsterdam. The story goes that on 15 March 1345, a dying man came to the priest for help and had administered to him his last sacraments. Nausea forced the Holy water back from whence it came, the man rather embarrassingly projectile-vomiting the Sacred Host into the fire. The Host, though, did not burn, He simply hovered above the flames. Cue the priest once more to retrieve the hovering ejectee and take Him back to the church, but all to no avail: He always managed to transport Himself back to the house. (I swear I am not making this up.) It eventually required an official procession back to the church to see to a restoration of peace and quiet, and the erecting of a chapel on the spot of the sick man's house (which later burned down). It became an object of worship, one still honoured today in the Silent Procession. The man with the dickey stomach lived to see another few years. As for the Church of St Nicholas, it is a feast of decoration: a more-than-worthwhile sight to behold. Though we know Saint Nicholas as the patron saint of children and Christmas, the people of

Amsterdam clung him hermetically to their bosom: his occasionally raucous lifestyle has immortalised him as, among other things, the patron saint of thieves and prostitutes too!

Westerkerk

Prinsengracht 279
Consecrated in 1631, this church is famous for being the place where Rembrandt is buried – problem is that no one knows exactly where. A flutter of academic excitement erupts every time a few old bones are found but the most likely explanation is that he was inadvertently excavated during some construction development (JCB say RIP!). A record of his burial on 8 Ocober 1669 does exist in the church register, but no plot was specified. A memorial plaque to honour his memory has been placed next to his son Titus's grave. A walk around the perimeter of this delightful church will take you to within view of where Descartes used to live (I think, therefore, that must be his house). Here, he who gave philosophy one of its most simple yet perplexing truisms wrote his *Treatise on the Passions of the Soul*. **Open** Monday-Friday 1100-1500

Westertoren

Prinsengracht 281 Phone **624 7766**
The Westerkerk was designed by Hendrick de Keyser (his son, Pieter saw the project through to completion after his father's death). De Keyser was the seventeenth-century 'Daddy' of Dutch architecture. He was single-handedly responsible for what is today known as the Amsterdam Renaissance style, though his influence extended internationally, well beyond the provinces of the city he so beautifully gave shape to. The tower, which opened seven years after the church, stands at a massive 280 feet high and contains the city's heaviest bell at 7,500kg. That's one big dong. During the 1940s, an engineer climbed out onto the top of the tower during a violent storm and with the help of his trusty theodolite managed to calculate that the tower swayed a massive three centimetres! During the summer months you too can ascend to the top for one of the most grandiose and underwear-browning views of the city available. **Open** Monday-Saturday 1000-1600 **Price** €1.75

Amstelkring Museum

Oudezijds Voorburgwal 40 Phone **624 6604**
Yes, technically a small museum, but this place is better known as Ons Lieve Heer Op Solder 'Our Lord In The Attic' (so that's where he is). You see, after the Reformation, during the seventeenth and eighteenth centuries, Catholic services were illegal. The authorities, however, did tend to turn a blind eye to what went on in the privacy of people houses, so long as they kept their activities away from the public eye. Local people held 'coventicles' (secret meetings) and adapted their houses with collapsible altars and switchable funiture. The attic in this house, the home of a former wealthy merchant of the 1660s was joined up with two other houses situated behind, and was consecrated as a church in 1663.Today, you can wander around the eighteenth- century reception room leading into the classic seventeenth- century Dutch sitting room, decked out with black and white symmetrical marble flooring and a massive walnut fireplace. Continue up through the bedrooms, up and up the small, wooden staircase, turn the corner at the top of the stairs

and... wow! Even for a heathen like me (who is sure to burn in hell), this sight is awesome. The paintings, the carvings, the altar and pulpit, the organ, and the sheer feeling of sorrow overwhelms you as you imagine how people, so strong in their beliefs, went to such lengths to continue with their faith despite it being against the law. **Open** Monday-Saturday 1000-1700. Sunday 1300-1700 **Price** €4.50

A few canals

Between 1650 and 1750, Amsterdam's population increased dramatically – nearly tenfold. The city's foresighted fathers though, had already been planning to push the city boundaries outwards with the introduction of three grand concentric canals: the Herengracht, the Keizersgracht and the Prinsengracht. These three main canals were intended for the richer elements of the population: for the bankers and merchants who wanted to live away from the harbour and its associated noises and smells. The shops and industries that were located in these prime areas were uprooted and banished to the poorer parts of the town. Amsterdam is much more water than these three canals alone though. There are 163 of them in total and they stretch just short of 50 miles around the city.

Herengracht

In his novel *The Fall*, The French novelist Albert Camus compared Amsterdam's Grachtengordel (girdle of canals) to the rings of hell. 'When one comes from the outside, as one gradually goes through those circles, life – and hence its crimes – becomes denser, darker. Here, we are in the last circle.' Well, life is certainly dense within the boundaries of this last circle, the Herengracht (literally the Gentleman's Canal, named after the gentleman who originally invested in it). It is dense with some of the city's finest and most opulent houses. Many of these can be found between Leidsestraat and Vijzelstraat, otherwise known as the 'Golden Bend'. Arguably though, the inhabitants of these houses are wealthier than the architecture. Decorating some of the other houses that line these waters you can spy dolphins, tigers and sea gods curling their way around sturdy gables; cornices curled with vine leaves and sprays of garlands mounted by urns; scatterings of pediments and pillars; sandstone vying with red brick. The Herengracht was the first canal to be dug in the city and most of the houses that fringe the canal date back to the eighteenth century. Among so many houses of distinction, then, you might consider stopping off at the Louis XIV building with curved balustrades at No. 475 that owns the reputation of 'Amsterdam's most beautiful house', or No. 605, the Museum Willet-Holthuysen, which is one of Amsterdam's most historic canal houses, splendidly replete with swish chandeliers on the inside and pristenely clipped hedges in its gardens. Or you could always moor up outside No. 52 for the cheekiest spliff of your visit – slap-bang in front of the city mayor's official residence.

Keizersgracht

The Keizersgracht (the Emperor's Canal, named after the Holy Roman Emperor Maximilian I) starts from Brouwersgracht (west of the station) and is a stretch of canal that contains numerous historical sights and attractions as well as being a gateway to side streets containing all manner of specialised shops. Along this circuit, at Keizersgracht 123, you'll come across the 'House with the Heads', so-called because of the three chiselled heads, each said to represent a classical god. Earnest whale-savers should carry on a bit further down the road for the headquarters of Greenpeace International. But, if bridges, and not whales, are your thing, then you should aim for the junction with Reguiliersgracht, where you can channel your view to see seven parallel bridges together. By night, this is one of the city's truly enchanting views.

Prinsengracht

This is the outer ring of the city's three grand concentric canals. It is the Prince's Canal, named after William, Prince of Orange. Bordering the Jordaan neighbourhood and stretching past Leidseplein, the tourist vortex of the city, to the south, and onto the Amstel River. Prinsengract is bordered by a rabbit run of side streets containing all sorts of speciality shops. This is probably the nicest of the canals for a leisurely stroll around: beautiful houses in leafy surroundings and lots of cafés that just beg you to sit down for a drink and imbibe the tranquility. Other places worth stopping off at are the Westerkerk, to take advantage of the stunning views from its tower, and the Woonbootmuseum, one of the biggest and most beautiful houseboats on Amsterdam's waters, worth adjourning to if only to sup a brisk cup of tea.

Oudezijds Voorburgwal

This used to be the canal that resided immediately inside the first city walls – hence *voor* (in front of). Today, this historical stretch is fenced by sex shops and myriad coffee shops, including the famous Bulldog coffee shop (famous only for being rude and expensive, in my humble opinion). Also along this stretch of waterway is the Anco Leather Hotel (see 'Accomodation' listing). Here too, you'll find the Huis op de Drie Grachten or House on the Three Canals. Why, you may ask, in a country that has more canal houses than Venice, is this one so special? Well, this happens to be the only one that lies at the corner of three canals. Look out for pretty red shutters that complement the green waters of Oudezijds Voorburgwal, Oudezijds Achterburgwal and Oudezijds Grimbergwal. You might also consider stopping off at the Amstelkring Museum for an idea of how clandestine worship at the time of the Reformation operated.

Oudezijds Achterburgwal

Running parallel with the Voorburgwal (collectively they are known as the Burgwallen) this canal runs through the *Rosse buurt* (that's the red-light district to you and me). Here you'll find an alarmingly eclectic mix of tourists, prostitutes, clergymen, children, druggies and those oh-so-priveleged residents – in short, Amsterdam in microcosm. This will give you as colourful and entertaining a glimpse of Amsterdam as anywhere else in the city. Whilst cruising or strolling this stretch, keep an eye out for the Erotic Museum and the Hash, Marijuana and Hemp Museum.

Klovenierburgwal

This canal, that runs south from Nieumarkt, was a fashionable address during the golden age of the seventeenth century, a time when the Dutch enjoyed an 'embarrassment of riches'. The most notable address here is that of No. 29, known as The Trippenhuis. This building belonged to two brothers – Louys and Hendrick Trip – who were fantastically rich and powerful arms dealers. Along with their rival, Louis De Geer, they controlled almost all of Europe's munitions supply. In a shameless display of wealth, the two brothers clubbed together to build two separate houses behind a vast, ornate single façade. A popular urban myth regarding this building goes on to describe a servant of the Trip brothers (or the coachman who delivered them to their new abode) commenting how she/he would be happy with a house the size of their front door. And so, the house across the canal at No. 26 is known as the Kleine Trippenhuis (Small Trip House). Built in 1696, it is one of the city's narrowest houses, only slightly broader at the back than it is at the front and it was claimed to have been built from the main house's leftover materials. The flaw of the story? Both brothers Trip were already dead by 1696. Hmmm.... Presently incumbent at Trip House is The Royal Netherlands Academy of Sciences, which has occupied the premises since 1887.

Geldersekade

North of Nieumarkt and terminating at St Nicolaaskerk, close to Centraal Station, is the Geldersekade Canal, besides which the old city wall used to run. Home nowadays to The Black Tulip Hotel (see 'Accommodation' listing) the area was notorious for its collection of bawdy drinking houses. A visiting seventeenth century-ambassador from Britain expressed his horror and further commentated '...there are tolerated in the city of Amsterdam, amongst other abuses, at least fifty music houses where lewd persons of both sexes meet to practice their villainies'. British ambassadors have been arriving in these parts with rude regularity ever since....

A few sights and attractions

You'd struggle to find as small but eclectic a city as this. You'll probably be fraught with trying to press as much as you can into your week or weekend. Before you set your itinerary in stone, make sure you've got a few of the following on your list.

The red-light district

This infamous and historical area borders Warmoesstraat to the west, Zeedijk to the north, Damstraat to the south and Kloveniersburgwal to the east. Surprisingly, this area has existed since the thirteenth century, a time when Amsterdam was starting out life as an important seat of maritime trade in the western world. An abundance of sailors started flooding into these parts and the profession of prostitution followed soon after. They supplied their services to this influx of 'lonely' sailors and to a variety of increasingly wealthy visitors. Unlike today, history shows that there were varying levels of tolerance to those that plied their trade with seafaring sorts. During the Alteration of 1578, prostitution was prohibited, but by the mid-seventeenth century, the government had relaxed its strong judiciary arm and adopted a more tolerant approach. In 1911, prostitution became legal throughout the Netherlands and in

2000, prostitution was finally removed from the statute books, making legal 'the world's oldest profession', finally free from prosecution. Today, the scene is as vibrant as ever. Even for those not interested in surreptitiously hiding the pork sword in the whore of their choice, this is a must-see part of The Dam. The red-light area has two completely different scenes. By day, the area looks like a 1930's side show, where hordes of tourists stand, leer and point at the women in the windows. It's characteristically seedy. As the dark veil of night descends, however, the area takes on a glamour and allure that is quite captivating. There's a hustle and energy that is infectious. Sure, it becomes a village for straight lads out to bag their sex souvenir of the city, with sex shops and sex clubs springing open in abundance, but you'll find a diverse cross section of people here and lots to see and do. Why not play 'Spot the boner' with your mates, counting the erections as they erupt from the trousers of the window-perusing straight boys getting all worked up over the chance of glimpsing a bit of Dutch pussy.

The Concertgebouw

Concertgebouwplein 2-6 Phone **671 8345**
Situated at the southern end of the Museumplein is the home of the Royal Concertgebouw Orchestra (RCO) which, since its foundation in 1888, has become famous as one of the world's leading symphony orchestras. Legend has it that the Concertgebouw might never have been, were it not for the rants of the visiting composer Brahms, who, in the 1870s, considered there to be not a single place in the city worthy of staging his music. Red-faced, various wealthy and important people of the city applied themselves to the task of darning this hole in their cultural sock, and the Concertgebouw was constructed little more than a decade later. Each Wednesday there is a free lunch concert at around 1230, although the queues start to build up by about noon. These are small recitals given in the small chamber music rooms in the upstairs part of the building, although, if you are lucky enough, you may be able to catch rehearsals in the main auditorium. Though the concert hall plays host to some of the world's finest composers and orchestras, there is a wide variety of seats and prices available, which could see you paying a mere few euros for your admission. **Open** (Box office) 1000-1900. Check listing magazines for current concerts and times **Price** €5-100+

Casa Rosso

Oudezijds Achterburgwal 106-108
Skip the sex shows that the world-famous Casa Rosso has on offer; just head here to take in (not literally, you understand) the huge marble-crafted penis fountain that stands proudly outside. A perfect photo opportunity ('Me and my giant cock') to show your folks back home.

Spinhuis

Oudezijds Achterburgwal 28
Back in the sixteenth century, an attempt to rehabilitate the lewd and incorrigible women of the night was made by forcing them, prison-like, to spin thread and make clothing for the poor. Like so many other things that look good on paper but fail miserably in practice, the idea of keeping such wicked women off the streets and divert their attentions from the good rogering they were most likely missing out on failed miserably.

The generous backhanders given to the custodians of the women by passing gentlemen callers persuaded a blind eye to be turned, and callers were soon dropping in to 'entertain' one or more of the women. A terracotta tableau above the door shows a workroom of women being beaten by a master with cat-o'-nine-tails in hand. Underneath, the inscription reads: *Cry not for I exact no vengeance for wrong, but force you to be good. My hand is stern but my heart is kind.* Yeah right, the dirty old bugger, he'd be paying a fortune for that sort of leather action down by the docks....

De Waag

Nieumarkt 4 Phone **422 7772**
Dominating the centre of Nieumarkt is the Disneyeque St Antoniespoort that began life in 1488 as one of the three main gates in the city wall (the other two being Reguliersspoort and Haarlemmerpoort). This spot was popular as the scene of many a public hanging and remnants of its gory past clearly remain on the south side of the building, where you can still see the bricked-up rectangles where the support beams of the gallows were slotted into. In 1617, the gate was converted into a public weighing house (De Waag), as all goods offloaded from the ships docked on the Geldersekade were weighed to determine their value and tax requirements. In the seventeenth century, the gate was adapted to house the dissecting room of the illustrious Guild of Surgeons. An ideal choice given that dead bodies were always close to hand, with public executions still routine in the area. It was also here that Rembrandt, at the age of 26, took anatomical lessons. From these he made sketches which would later form the basis for his famous *The Anatomy Lesson of Dr Nicolaes Tulp*. In the following years, DeWaag was used as a fire station and also as the starting point for subsequent museums (the Amsterdam Historical Museum and the Jewish Historical Museum). From 1989 to 1994, the building was empty, but in 1992 renovation work began to turn the building into a restaurant downstairs (Café De Waag) and a Society for Old and New Media upstairs.

In't Aepjen

Zeedijk 1
This timber house is one of the oldest buildings in the city and one of two remaining wooden buildings in central Amsterdam. It was built in 1550 as a seaman's hostel, where sailors who had drunk or gambled away their money were allowed to leave their pet monkeys in lieu of payment. Obviously, the place got infested with fleas and mites, not to mention being overrun with monkeys, and so, the place became known as In't Aepjen, quite literally, 'in the monkeys'. Scratching seamen would betray the details of where they had slept the night before. Today they are remembered by this place and a saying still in circulation that refers to someone who is in financial difficulty as having '*in de aap gelogeerd*' (stayed in the monkey). This tiny bar still has 1920s music-hall wall panels and other antiquities worth a gawp. **Open** Daily 1500-0100

National Liberation Monument

Dam Square
Standing proud at the eastern edge of the square is the towering, phallic National Liberation Monument. It is the picture many people conjure when they think of Amsterdam. It was erected on 4 May in 1956 as a

memorial to honour the Dutch victims of the Second World War. Inside the 21-metre obelisk are eleven urns containing soil from each of the Netherlands' provinces. There is a further urn containing soil from the war graves of the Dutch East Indies, a Dutch colony until 1949. During the sixties it became a sort of hippy totem pole, with the summer months seeing hundreds of long-haired meditative sorts adapting the raised platforms and surrounding areas as makeshift accommodation. Police and local authorities made several attempts to remove them by using fire hoses to wash them away, but this led to protest riots. In the early seventies a group of marauding marines reputedly chased away the hippies forever. Today, the monument and square serves as a central hub and meeting spot for the hordes of tourists who pass through this section of the city each year.

Koninklijk Paleis

Dam Square Phone **620 4060**
Occupying the entire western end of the square is the Royal Palace, formerly the Stadhuis (city hall) until 1808 when King Louis Bonaparte decided he wanted to live here. Upon his words it was redesigned to reflect the home of the monarchy. It has remained the Royal Palace ever since but Queen Beatrix never spends the night here, except for official receptions, preferring the Huis ten Bosch in the Hague. One of the most interesting aspects of the building's exterior is the lack of any kind of grand entrance. The seven archways that allow access into the building from street level have no steps. Before Bonaparte's reign, this indicated that the town hall belonged to everyone, that they could literally walk in off the streets. Whilst the outside of the building may not be as grand and imposing as its European counterparts, the inside is a completely different story. The Burgerzaal (Citizen's Hall) is a vast space designed to be the universe contained in a single room. The walls are encrusted with marble carvings and reliefs that glint in the light that pours in from all sides. Rows of monolithic crystal chandeliers hang from the distant ceiling like the stars and stunning brass inlaid maps on the floor show the heavenly and terrestrial worlds. Amsterdam, not surprisingly, is at the centre, with the enthroned maid of the city proudly surveying over it all. **Open** June-August: Monday-Sunday 1100-1730 **Price** €4.75

Gate of the Rasphuis

Voetboogstraat
Nip down the side street from Spuistraat and have a gander at this remarkable gate. It was the former entrance of what was the male equivalent of the Spinhuis. Accordingly then, it was for ne'er-do-well naughty boys who, in order to purge their souls and to prevent them from having impure thoughts, were set a collection of mundane and often back-breaking tasks. One example was the sawing of wood into a fine powder to make dyes with. If the boys refused to do the set work they were placed into a water tub where they had to pump away a continuous flow of water lest they would drown.

Tuschinski Cinema

26-28 Reguliersbreestraat Phone **626 2633**
Lovers of art deco will absolutely cream their pants (as art aficionados would say) at the internal and external grandeur of this absolutely glori-

ous building. Situated on the short strip between Muntplein and Rembrandtplein, the Tuschinski is acknowledged as one of the greatest and most beautiful cinemas in the world. Abraham Tuschinski, a Jewish refugee from Poland, saw his first film in 1910 and immediately wanted his own cinema. He didn't want any old cinema, though. Oh no. He wanted a place where his 'guests' could 'lose themselves in another world'. And so, eleven years later in 1921, wealthy enough to fulfil his dream, he set about building what you see today. The cinema has just undergone a massive and costly refurbishment which has brought the cinema bang up-to-date in modern technology and comfort, whilst preserving its stunning interiors. Every decorative detail has been lovingly cleaned, repaired and restored to its original glory and mile upon mile of plumbing and electrical wiring have been replaced. Eighty years of nicotine stains and popcorn grease have vanished from the walls, and so too the modern wallpaper – stripped away to reveal art deco women painted onto the wall that no one knew existed. **Price** €4-8 (guided tour at €4.50)

Holland Experience

Waterlooplein 17 Phone **422 2233**
Directly next to Rembrandhuis, this attraction, though expensive for what it is, provides a welcome break if you're suffering from culture overload. This 30-minute 3D scene-arama takes you around the Netherlands in an all-out assault of sensual stimulation. It sprays you with water at the mere sight of H_2O reservoirs (particularly the dam bust), and it sprays perfume into the auditorium when you go over the flower fields. Throughout it all, the seating platform shudders with unerring regularity. In the name of true simulation of a whirlwind trek through the country, I was hoping for a breeze through the red-light district complete with an artificially rendered blow job... 'twas not to be. It must be said that the 'Experience' does paint the country a shade duller than the street you've just stepped in off (Disney ride conoisseurs take note), but it gets you away from all the crowds for a bit and you can still go home bragging about how you and some other guy felt the ground shake as you got wet and smelly together. **Open** Monday-Sunday 1000-1800 (first show starts at 1030, then every hour on the hour until 1700, through until the last show at 1730) **Price** €8

Desmet Cinema

Plantage Middenlaan 4 Phone **627 3434**
An ornately decorated art deco cinema reminiscent of the Kit Kat Club in Cabaret. During the Second World War, German Jewish refugees put on staged theatre and cabaret shows that were so unwittingly popular that many Nazi officers in charge of deportation came to watch. Today, the cinema is known for its imaginative gay screenings and mini festivals. **Open** (check listings magazines for current screenings)

The House with the Heads

Keizersgracht 123
The House with the Heads was built in 1622 for the rich merchant Nicholaas Sohier. In 1634, Sohier sold the house to Louis de Geer, an arms dealer who owned several iron mines in Sweden and maintained close connections with the Swedish king, Gustav Adolf. The House with the Heads is one of only three surviving early-seventeenth-century hous-

es with additional wings, the predecessor of the double canal house. (The other members of this group are the 'Dolphin' at Singel 140-142 and the 'Bartolotti House' at Herengracht 170-172.) The six heads from which the house derives its name are prominently displayed. They represent divinities from classical antiquity: Apollo with his laurel wreath occurs twice (the two heads on the far left and far right); Diana, the moon goddess with the crescent; Ceres with her ears of corn; Bacchus with his bunch of grapes; while Minerva and Mars (the war god with helmet) are depicted on either side of the entrance gate. Legend has it that these are in actual fact the heads of six robbers, decapitated by a fearless maid servant!

Magere Brug

A small, narrow bridge spanning the Amstel at the eastern end of the Prinsengracht. The 'Skinny Bridge' was built in the seventeenth century for two spoilt, young women who were too lazy to walk the long way round from their house on Kerkstraat to their stables across the river. The other interpretation of the story contains the same two sisters, but tells it that they lived opposite each other on the river and had the bridge built in order to make the passage between their two homes a little easier. Either way, lazy cows. When the time came in 1934 to replace the original rotting bridge with a metal structure there was a public outcry. The city relented, and provided the town with a replica of the original. The bridge is illuminated each evening with thousands of lights, making it a popular location for both lovers and photographers. Just down from the Magere Brug and in the river opposite the eastern end of the Prinsengracht is a barrier of 'sluice gates'. Each night between 1900 and 2030 two burly men crank the wooden wheels that close them. At the other far eastern side of the city on the island of Zeeburg, a pumping station starts up and forces 600,000 cubic metres of water into the city's canals, forcing the old water out through sluices in the west. This helps to eradicate the smell of stagnating water from the canals which in bygone days was overpowering, even at a time when townsfolk had stopped using the canal system as a sewer. Indeed, many people today do still use the canals for their 'wild pissing' activities (but that's another long story).

Carre Theatre

Amstel 115 Phone **622 5225**

Across the Amstel, at the start of Nieuwe Prinsengracht, there is a delightfully classical building with a cornice of happy smiling clowns and grinning jesters. This is the Carre Theatre, built as a circus for Oscar Carre in 1887. Every year in September, until 1875, Amsterdam had held an annual fair. It was a three-week affair that consumed the whole city with celebrity appearances, dances, side shows and circuses. One of these circuses was Carre's, to which King William had granted the honorary title of 'Royal Dutch' – a royal sign of approval. As the years went by, the long periods of revelry proved to be a little too much for the Protestant patricians and the city council ensured 'the Kermis of 1875' was to be the last. Despite ferocious street rioting , the edict was carried out and the city lost its annual piss-up! Carre, however, decided he was going to stay and built a temporary wooden tent structure beside the Amstel, later adding a stone façade. Outraged, the council demanded that he tear it down, but Carre fought it out and eventually got his way. The building you see today was constructed in a matter of months as the permanent home of the circus. It now hosts a variety of shows, but always reverts back to its origins with a circus during the Christmas period.

Homomonument **Corner of Westermarkt and Keizergracht**

The Homomonument was created in 1987 by Karin Daan to commemorate the gay men and lesbians who died in the Second World War. The monument consists of three pink granite triangles representing past, present and future, which together form one bigger triangle. The inscription on the monument reads, *Commemorating all women and men ever oppressed and persecuted because of their homosexuality*. Incidentally, this is only one of two homosexual monuments in the world – the other is a spare brass plaque outside Berlin's Nollendorfplatz U-Bahn. There are three annual events held at the monument each year: Queens Day on 30 April; Remembrance Day on 5 May and an event to commemorate the unveiling of the monument, which takes place each 5 September. Each time the memorial is adorned with flowers.

Vrouwen van Ravensbrück Memorial **Museumplein**

A memorial to commemorate the women who died in concentration camps during the Second World War. The memorial is a series of vertical steel slabs surrounding a circular obelisk and was constructed in 1975 by Joost van Santen and is dedicated to the women of Ravensbrück. It incorporates a beating soundtrack and flickering lights intended to 'call' people to the monument and continue the fight against fascism. The text on the monument reads, *For those women who until the bitter end refused to accept fascism*.

A few shops

Amsterdam is a pleasure to shop in, mostly because you don't have to walk miles while you are doing it. The majority of the shopping areas are compact and full of small, individual shops – be they selling diamonds or mineral water. For the more routine shopping expedition, there is also a main core of large retail units at Nieuwendiijk/Kalverstraat around Dam Square. This is open every day and gets really crowded, especially on Sunday. If it's raining then opt for the mall-like Magna Plaza. This splendidly striped building was once the post office but has now been filled with an excellent selection of shops. Fashion in the Netherlands tends to be understated and focused on the traditional mainstays of quality and cut. It is not outspoken, nor does it shamelessly cry out for attention. If you are looking for international designer clothing and shoes then visit Koningsplein and Leidsestraart. If interiors are your thing then the Netherlands is internationally acclaimed for its designs and there are some excellent furniture shops in the Rozengracht in the Jordaan. For food, head for The Pijp, with lots of ethnic food stores as well as the Albert Cyp market. On Saturdays visit the Boerenmarket –

the farmers' market – in Noorderkstraat in the Jordaan. During the summer, on Sunday, if you'd rather mingle than shop, then mosey through the arts and craft stalls in Spui, where the buskers will keep you entertained in between your browsing. If you are really pushed for time just head for the Jorddan – for a jigsaw-box photograph of how you imagined Amsterdam to be. This is a really attractive area of back streets and canals which are a delight to walk through anyway, but here there is the bonus of some of the city's more individual, if not downright quirky, shops to boot. Beware your shopping instincts leading you down to the red-light district, for this is one area where a leisurely approach to window shopping could well pass off the wrong signals.

Amsterdam has wonderful markets: flea markets, second-hand clothing, antiques, flowers, food. All of them are great places for bargain hunting and for mixing it with the rest of the city. Definitely worth rummaging through is the Waterlooplein, which has amazing hand-me-downs on show. The Looier at Elandsgracht 109 is an antique hunter's delight. Lots of stalls, not so much hubble and hassle perhaps, but lots of quality browsing (but closed on Fridays). With the Netherlands' involvement in the floral industry, the flower markets are not to be missed. Even though the Bloemenmarkt at Singel is more of a show for tourists now than a working market, don't miss out on these barges laden with the lushest, plumpest flowers. And yes, you can bring back tulips from Amsterdam (I think I feel a song coming on), but no, not gladioli or chrysanthemums.

Night shops are the Dutch equivalent of the 'Mother-forgot' corner shop, except that you're unlikely to bump into your mother here. Pricey, but there for those midnight panics, and they usually stay open until 0100 and some right throughout the night. The most exclusive and expensive is Heuft's in Rinjstraat, perfect for curing that midnight hankering for an oyster or two.

Being a pedestrian in Amsterdam can be unbelievably disconcerting. You get the hang of cars, that stop at red lights; get the hang of those trams, that sort of swing around; but bikes: bikes are silent and deadly! Rather naively, one assumes a heirarchy where two legs have more rights than two wheels. Forget it. Bikes rule. Don't get in their way, and their riders will pedal by with a smile. Trespass on a bike lane, though, and, by law, you are regarded as a heinous nuisance. The only way to understand this passion for spokes then, is to try it – and you too will fall in love with your big-wheeled, solid-framed, extremely upright and uptight bike. Whizzing along, being rude to every pedestrian that dares set foot within an inch of your territory will soon become second nature. You can rent bikes from most stations, particularly Centraal Station, and a good selection of bikes to rent or buy is available at Bike City, Bloemgracht 70.

De Bijenkorf

De Bijenkorf Dam 1, Old Centre Phone **621 8080**
This is the main-stay department store of Amsterdam and it's busy (De Bijenkorf translates as The Beehive). Everything is here, including a sep-

arate department, The Chill Out, for those not looking for that latest designer must-have but merely for the latest street-style buzz. A very useful can-probably-find it-there sort of place. If the shopping bags begin to weigh you down this is also a good place to set down for lunch. De Bijenkorf is open every day but not until 1100 on Mondays, and 1200 on Sundays.

Wegewijs Rozengracht 32 Phone 624 4093

If your knowledge of Dutch cheese is limited to that which is round and red then visit the Wegewijs. This family have been in cheese for generations and have an extensive display of cheeses from all over the world, not just the Netherlands. Unfortunately, or fortunately, you might have to eat it all before you leave as export to some countries is a customs no-no.

Huize van Wely Beethovenstraat 72 Phone 662 2009

The secret is now out – the Dutch make staggeringly good chocolate. Hopefully you'll already have discovered the sublime charms of Dutch hot chocolate with a hefty whack of whipped cream. Here you will delight in exquisitely delicious handmade chocolates to rival any you would find across in neighbouring Belgium.

Simon Levelt Prinsengracht 180 Phone 624 0823

Chocolate, tobacco and tea were but three of those early drugs unleashed on a bewildered Dutch public centuries ago. The other was coffee. This magnificently tiled spendour is as gorgeous a place to buy it as you'll find in the whole of Europe. Closed on Monday morning.

Condomerie Het Guiden Vlies Warmoesstraat 141 Phone 627 4174

Every conceivable gimmick has here been utilised to enhance the humble condom. Ah, where would we be without them? They glow, they smell (couldn't find any pine-forest floor, but I'm sure they're here somewhere), and – this is the science bit – they come in a lot of sizes (mine included). This is a serious condom shop, well worth checking out if only to suppress your rubbery titters when trying out the measuring guide (I kid ye not).

Big Shoe Leliegracht 12 Phone 622 6645

You know what they say about men with big feet. Well, in the hope of finding 'him', I ventured over to Big Shoe and found... only shoes that were big. Never mind, for this is definitely the place to come if you have ever been pinned in or pushed out by the sizist shoe fraternity. Big Shoe is fantastic and carries a good stock of shoes for both men and women, with no need to be shy about your size. A top treat for those who know the ordeal of covering large southern extremities.

Wooden Shoe Factory Nieuwe Hoogstraat 11 Phone 427 3862

Racks and racks of colourfully decorated wooden shoes – with straps, without straps, with flowers, without flowers, with windmills... you get the picture: lots of choice. If you don't think you'll be a fan, you will be. This is the home of some beautifully crafted footwear. Clogtastic.

De Witte Tandenwinkel

Runstraat 5 Phone **623 3443**
Everything for the teeth in your life – not just brushes and flosses, but the ultimate in dental decadence. Rinses and powders, things that polish and preen and gadgets so strange you'll be afraid to ask what they do do. A real mouth-opener and an absolute necessity if you stopped off at Huize van Wely on the way.

Absolute Danny

Oudezijds Achterburgwal 78 Phone **421 0915**
In case you couldn't find what you were looking for at De Witte Tandenwinkel then try here. Try not to be distracted by the – mostly black and shiny – clothing, head instead for their rather unique line in exotic toothbrushes.

Clubwear House

Herengracht 265 Phone **622 8766**
A brilliant place for catching up with Dutch fashion and to try on their own label, Wearhouse 2000. This is also a great place to pick up clubbing info and tickets. If you like a buzz when you shop then come here on Saturday when DJs whip up an atmosphere of shopping frenzy.

Midtown

Nieuwendijk 104 Phone **638 4252**
Amsterdam has a great range of niche music stores dotted along its many side streets. This is just one of them, specialising in dance music and its many manifestations, from house to hardcore and garage to trance. This is also a good place for picking up information and tickets for events.

Backbeat Records

Egelantiersstraat 19 Phone **627 1657**
Another specialist shop, this one run by an enthusiast who prefers the mellower side of discs and vinyl. There's a great collection of jazz and blues, from the classics right through to contemporary artists.

Metz & Co

Keizersgracht 455 Phone **520 7020**
You might not have intended to shop for designer furniture but all that could change. In this department store, on the corner of Leidsestraat and Keizersgracht, there is a gorgeous selection of modern furniture, including some inspiring Dutch designs. There is also a good display of contemporary ceramics, if you fancy a souvenir more swish than the 'I did the Dam' two-euro mug. The store is lavishly presented, but if it's real jaw-dropping scenery you're after, then take the elevator up to the sixth-floor café for one of the best views out over the city.

Kitsch Kitchen

Rozengracht 183 Phone **622 8261**
Stacked high and overflowing with fantastic fantasies of colourful plastic. Woeful wicker baskets and nightmarish bygone wallpapers. This is Retro Heaven for those with a phobia of the sleek and simple. I mean, who could bear to be without a bright pink chandelier in their lives? Hmmm... tread carefully, make eye contact with none of the staff and you might just get out of here as a wisened voyeur, rather than an out-of-pocket consumer convert. Keep your sunglasses on and prepare to be dazzled.

Holland Gallery de Munt

Munttoren, Muntplein 12 Phone **623 2271**
If you've just ventured in from Kitsch Kitchen, then take off your sunglasses and sift through this wealth of Amsterdam souvenirs, all without a whiff of day-glo to them. Delve through selections of antique Delftware and hand-painted tiles and bring back something that will put a smile of appreciation on mother's chops.

Lambiek

Kerkstraat 78 Phone **626 7543**
This is a haven for comic buffs. As well as having a vast array of old and new comics from all over the world, there is a programme of exhibitions that feature renowned cartoonists.

Hemp Works

Nieuwendijk 13 Phone **421 1762**
If you don't fancy smoking or eating it, then why not wear it? It actually looks rather good, not at all hairy and sandley. Great casual hemp shirts and jeans. You can also wash in it and accerorise with it. Do you know, I'm starting to see the old rope in a completely different light.

A few coffeeshops

Well, I could hardly give you a whistle-stop tour of the city without mentioning a coffeeshop or two, now could I? There are more than 300 such institutions lining the streets and back streets of the capital. If you're strapped for cash for your hash then try and avoid frequenting those shops based in the tourist areas. If, however, you've got plenty in the pot to spend on your pot then you can do no better than sampling the unique atmosphere of those wiffy wacky-baccy shops that lie at the heart of the city. Here's several of the best, and if you can make it round half of them, then you're a better man than me. Warning: after leaving any of these establishments, rest for at least two hours before attempting to visit Kitsch Kitchen.

Greenhouse

Oudezijds Voorburgwal 191 Phone **627 1739**
If you have no idea about any of this coffeehouse culture, then you can do far worse than sticking to places where someone does. The Greenhouse is littered with awards for its cannabis, so you can relax and slide into the sofa with confidence. This is a legend among coffeeshops and patroned by connoisseurs and celebrities alike (the Rolling Stones like to get stoned here, not to mention Quentin Tarantino). Hippies, backpackers and intellectual-looking sorts make up the rest of the clientele. It's a bit out from the centre, but the Number 4 Tram will get you out here. You can sort out getting back later. Now, what shall I start with...?

The Otherside

Regliersdwarsstraat 6 Phone **421 1014**
This is where, as the Dutch put it, 'those from the other side like to contemplate the otherness of their being'. Yes, well, if that doesn't give you a clue as to the potency of some of the leaves and buds on sale here then I don't know what will. This is, at present, the only gay coffeeshop in the city. A must-visit place.

Paradox

1E Bloemdwarsstraat 2 Phone **623 5639**
For those who prefer eating from the table to slipping under it. You can gorge on delicious health food, from hemp burgers to freshly squeezed juices, and then, when all is done, take a toke or three as digestive juices go about their business. Paradox is a cheery change from the stained, stoned coffeeshop model.

De Rokerij

Lange Leidsedwarsstraat 41 Phone **622 9442**
Welcome to a hip hippies' coffeeshop, where elephants on the walls, melodious harmonising music, candles and sweeping extractor fan blades all start to swirl in a smokey, convivial environment, awash with fellow joint suckers. Drinks and tasty treats could easily entice you into reclining for a few pleasant hours here.

Katsu

Eerste van der Helstraat 70
A shop with no phone, website or promotional gimmicks, just high quality, high-strength grass. Katsu were among the first to start selling Haze strains that were doing the rounds in California back in the eighties. It makes for a sweet and odorous smoke and the locals seem to love it. Among the locals on show are a non-smoking octogenarian who comes here daily! Whereas other coffee shops in the area attract mainly tourists, Katsu has a distinct family air to it, one in which you can relax and take in the sixties music and sweet, hazy smell.

Barney's

Haarlemmerstraat 102 Phone **625 9761**
Fry-ups followed by skinning up. Not sure quite who Barney is but he is obvously one for getting up early (this place opens at 0700). He's also as famous for his fantastic anytime breakfasts (full-English or a veggie/vegan alternative) as he is for his joints of prize-winning grass. Come and rub shoulders with other lovers of grease and greens.

Rusland

Rusland 14-16 Phone **627 9468**
A squeaky and creaky house, but one of the most comfy and spacious coffeeshops you'll come across during your stay. This was one of Amsterdam's first coffeeshops not to do coffee (the sticker in the window proudly claims 'Coffeeshop #001'). These days you *can* pick up coffee or choose from a staggering variety of teas, as well as a tasty selection of snacks and, of course, an excellent selection of good-price hash. Whilst here, look to make the acquaintance of resident feline 'Rambo'.

De Dampkring

Handboogstraat 29 Phone **638 0705**
Don't be distracted by the pubby feel and the drinks being served. Ask for the menu which helpfully catagorises in degrees of 'highness' – be it clear, psychedelic or plain old heavily-stoned. If the hash doesn't cut it for you, then indulge instead on the menu of available munchies – from *tostis*, brownies and muffins to yogurt with muesli.

Grey Area

Oude Leliestraat 2 Phone **420 4301**
Another of the original coffeeshops, with a long list of celebrity patrons (when in Amsterdam, Woody from *Cheers* likes to prop himself up on

the other side of the bar here). Grey Area is actually as unlike *Cheers* as you can get, with determined anti-designer touches. Its marketing zeal, however, is one that most of the coffeeshops shy away from, though the publicity machine is not all of its own making (there's an unofficial fan website!). So, if you can cope with all the hype and you don't mind rubbing shoulders with Hollywood A-listers or faces from MTV, head here and find great staff, a prize-winning menu and a fridge full of shatteringly cold soft drinks.

A few restaurants

Amsterdam cuisine? A glut of hamburger chains, streets lined with bakeries, window-cum-serving-hatches spewing forth hot croissants and savoury pastries to eat on the go. Or the Dutch delicacy – *nieuwe haring* – raw, pickled herring served with onions to swallow in one, head tipped back, like a gannet would down his catch. Or *frikandel*, the famous Dutch sausage. It's hardly the most edifying prospect for the well-travelled gastronome, is it? True, generally speaking, Dutch cuisine is hardly likely to set the taste buds on fire, but the country's colourful colonial past has ensured that a wide variety of ethnic eateries can be found in the capital city. Notably, there's a strong Indonesian scene, with Chinese and Surinamese flavours also popular. Amsterdam may not have the strength in depth of, say, London or Paris but even so, the hungry, gay gastronaut should be able to find plenty of excellent restaurants to choose from. The Dutch are up-late-folk who have dinner between 1900 and 2100, during which times restaurants are at their busiest. The list below should guide you to a few of the best eateries in the city. *Eet smakelijk* (enjoy your food).

De Silveren Spiegel

Kattengat 4 Phone **624 6589**
One of Amsterdam's most highly regarded and consistently reliable restaurants, specialising in what could loosely be termed Dutch cuisine, with a strong emphasis on fish. **Price** Expensive

Christophe

Leliegracht 46 Phone **625 0807**
You will need to book early to ensure getting a table at this Michelin-starred restaurant, which sits overlooking the pretty Leliegracht. Cooking of the highest quality in a romantic and civilised setting. A well-chosen wine list complements the Provençal-cum-North-African-influenced dishes. Just the place for a special occasion. **Price** Expensive

Shiva

Reguliersdwarsstraat 72 Phone **624 8713**
Amsterdam has a number of good Indian restaurants and this is one of the best. Excellent-value authentic regional dishes dominate the menu, including a wide selection of vegetarian options. **Price** Cheap

Samo Sebo

P. C. Hoofstraat 27 Phone **662 8146**
It's Indonesian food that has really put Amsterdam on the culinary map and Samo Sebo has long been regarded as the finest exponent of this sub-

tle and addictive cuisine. The *rigsttafel* (a banquet of rice and exquisite side dishes) is outstanding. **Price** Moderate

Rosa's Cantina

Reguliersdwarsstraat 38 Phone **625 9797**
This is just a great place to people-watch. Always packed and buzzing, with crowds overflowing onto the terrace. A no-reservations policy means that the bar gets very cramped with thirsty revellers demanding margaritas and tequilas like there's no tomorrow. The Tex-Mex inspired food isn't bad either. **Price** Cheap-moderate

Pier 10

De Ruyterkade, Pier 10 Phone **624 8276**
A restaurant hidden behind Centraal Station on the pier – ideal for those romantic, last-night, candlelit meals. If you're keen on one of the large-picture-window tables then be sure to book ahead. You'll then be able to sit down and taste the delights of this pleasant and affordable international menu. **Price** Moderate

Inez ISPC

Amstel 2 Phone **639 2899**
An international menu awaits those that find this place. Others will more than likely pass by its inconspicuous exterior. Once in, you'll find food that's expensive but worth every cent and great service. Lunches are particularly busy, so reserve a table before making the trek. **Price** Moderate-expensive

Le Pecheur

Reguliersdwarsstraat 32 Phone **624 3121**
A truly great restaurant, especially if you are lucky enough to nab one of the tables on the lovely terrace outside. Fish is probably what Amsterdam does best and no restaurant does it better than Le Pecheur. **Price** Moderate-expensive

1e Klas

Centraal Station Phone **625 0131**
There is something very romantic about old-style railway restaurants and this turn-of-the-century art nouveau gem is no exception. The menu here offers everything from excellent sandwiches right up to a full à la carte menu. The perfect place to while away the time before setting off on your journey. **Price** Cheap-moderate

L'Angoletto

Hemonystraat 18 Phone **676 4182**
This is Amsterdam's favourite Italian restaurant. Expect long waits for the ever-popular tables (due to their no-bookings policy). But this merely builds the excitement and helps ensure there is always a buzzing, expectant atmosphere. Good standard fare with most diners opting for the ever reliable pizza and pasta dishes. **Price** Cheap

Temp Doeloe

Utrechtsestraat 75 Phone **625 6718**
Popular and highly-regarded Indonesian that serves some of the most imaginative spiced food in town. Be warned: some of the dishes are very hot indeed, so be sure to consult with your waiter before ordering. Book ahead, as tables are hard to come by here. **Price** Moderate

Duende **Lindengracht 62** Phone **420 6692**

Wonderful tapas can be found here at this small and friendly bar-restaurant in the Jordaan district. Dishes are displayed at the bar so just go up and order and then take your drink to a table and wait for them to appear. When they have all disappeared, as they quickly will, it's back up to the bar to order some more... **Price** Cheap

Borderwijk **Noordermarkt 7** Phone **624 3899**

Undoubtedly one of Amsterdam's leading restaurants, serving perfectly executed French dishes with style and aplomb in a pleasingly contemporary setting. You will need to book well in advance to secure a table. **Price** Moderate-expensive

Café Americain **Leidseplein 97** Phone **624 5322**

An Amsterdam institution and a serious draw for locals and tourists alike. The glamorous art deco interior ensures that this is also a destination for the glitterati. Open from breakfast onwards. **Price** Cheap-moderate

El Rancho **Reguliersdwarsstraat 8** Phone **625 0592**

Situated in the city's premier gay street, nowhere else demonstrates the Dutch's love of all things meat in such bold print. This is an Argentinian steakhouse chain for those with a big appetite. Tamer sorts should go for a starter only, but chest-beating carnivores should settle for no less than the Paradilla, a mixed meat platter served on a table grill. **Price** Cheap-moderate

Huyschkaemer **Utrechtsestraat 137** Phone **627 0575**

This is a popular, cheerful gay and lesbian modern diner, with a good choice of main courses including a reasonable vegetarian selection. You may find your metabolism accelerated by the weekend DJs. **Price** Cheap

The guide

Bars

Amstel Taveerne

Amstel 54, 1017 AB Phone **623 4254**
A bar as popular with the locals as it is with the tourists, which in my book is always a good sign. This was the first gay bar in the Amstel area and no doubt it was as popular then as it is today. The Amstel is a lively and exceptionally friendly place where the locals, huddling around the semicircular bar, will be genuinely interested in you and your tales. Drunken and good-humoured 'Tulips from Amsterdam' sing-along sessions are practically guaranteed over the weekend although you will have to get here early as the place gets crammed from the pool tables right to the front door. Beer mugs and knick-knacks hang gracefully from the beams, reproduction old masters grace the walls and jocular locals perch on 'their' stools around the bar, waiting to see what tourist foibles they will be subjected to tonight. **Open** Sunday-Thursday 1600-0100. Friday-Saturday 1500-0300

Anco Bar

Oudezijds Voorburgwal 55, 1012 EJ Phone **624 1126**
Web **www.ancohotel.nl**
Men-only leather bar with a hotel above the premises (see Anco Hotel under Accommodation). With its welcoming bar and well-used darkroom at the back of the premises, the Anco is renowned for being sleazy, sexual and hardcore, but the punters would not have it any other way. **Open** Monday-Sunday 0900-2200

April

Reguliersdwarsstraat 37 1017 BK Phone **625 9572**
A modern and trendy bar used as either an overflow from the slightly more popular Soho across the street or a pit stop for cruisers ensuring they have not missed any fresh meat on their trek down this famous strip. Everyone who has been here tends to remember the revolving back bar (and the steep bar prices). At the weekend the bar is near to bursting point although the constant toing and froing between here and Soho means that if you stay in one place you will see all the men on the pull without moving a muscle. **Open** Sunday-Thursday 1400-0100. Friday-Saturday 1400-0300

Argos

Warmoesstraat 95, 1012 HZ Phone **622 6595**
E-mail **leather@argosbar.demon.nl**
Once you get through those dark curtains you are in the land of heavy leather and no-holds-barred sex. Make your way along the balcony and then head down to the cellar where a catacomb of darkrooms and passageways will ensure that you bump into loads of interesting people. Argos is regarded as the oldest leather bar in Europe (some of the punters look as though they have been here since opening day) and the premier gay man's leather bar – one that boasts a ubiquitous collection of slings, hoists and other paraphernalia. See also Sex on Sunday @ Argos under 'Clubs and club nights'. **Open** Sunday-Thursday 2200-0300. Friday-Saturday 2200-0400

Back Door Café

Amstelstraat 32, 1017 DA Phone **620 2333** Web **www.backdoor.nl/cafe**
The café-bar part of this bar and club set-up. A nice, young, fun-loving crowd gets together in this rather smart and laid-back café-bar situated just by Rembrandtplein. For club nights held at the Back Door Club, see the listings for Coco Latté, Heat and the Sunday Tea Dance under 'Clubs and club nights'. **Open** Wednesday-Thursday 1700-0100. Friday-Saturday 1700-0300. Sunday 1700-0100

Camp Café

Kerkstraat 45, 1017 GB Phone **622 1506**
A café-bar that is at its busiest during the evening, full of people about to spend a night in Thermos Night. An ideal resting spot in the day if you've been evicted from the sauna or need to rest your weary bones. **Open** 0800-0100 (food served 1000-2330)

Casa Maria

Warmoesstraat 60, 1012 JG Phone **627 6848**
Very popular locals' bar, probably because of the cheap drinks and interesting crowd. Situated in the the heart of the red-light district, the big picture window ensures that people-watching – particularly the young straight boys visiting the local prossies – remains the in-house sport! Very friendly and an ideal place to take a break from the hustle and bustle of this busy stretch of the city. **Open** Sunday-Thursday 1200-0100. Friday-Saturday 1200-0300

Café Chris

Bloemstraat 42 1016 LC Phone **624 5942**
Not a gay bar but interesting for being one of the oldest bars in Amsterdam – along with a number of others where, conveniently, no categorical proof exists! This place has been a taphouse since 1624, where the builders of the nearby Westerkerk (Western Church) are said to have gone to receive their wages. One of the curiosities of this bar's interior is the toilet, which is flushed from behind the bar *outside* the lavatory. If the barman is in fine fettle he can be persuaded to flush the toilet while your 'friend in the John' is still erm . . . contemplating. Worth popping in if you are in the area near the Flower Market.

Club Jacques

Warmoesstraat 93, 1012 HZ Phone **622 0323**
Next door to Argos, this small leather-and-jeans bar tends to get very busy as the evening progresses. The promise of uncomplicated, no-strings sex in the adjoining darkroom keeps the punters coming back for more. **Open** Sunday-Thursday 2000-0300. Friday-Saturday 2100-0400

Cock and Feathers

Zeedijk 23-25 Phone **624 3141**
An intimate and cosy little bar and restaurant across the strip from the Queen's Head. Food served daily from 1800. **Open** Sunday-Thursday 1700-0100. Friday-Saturday 1700-0200

Cosmo Bar

Kerkstraat 42, 1017 GM Phone **624 8074**
A relaxed but exceptionally busy bar attached to the Amistad (formerly Westend) Hotel. The late-night opening hours provide welcome respite and alcohol prior to visiting Thermos Night. **Open** Sunday-Thursday 1600-0300. Friday-Saturday 0100-0400

Cuckoo's Nest

Nieuwezijds Kolk 6, 1012 PV Phone **627 1752**
A men-only leather bar situated off Niewendijk, deemed to have one of Amsterdam's largest playrooms/darkrooms in the basement. Best in the afternoon and late evening, which means it is a good place to start and end a day of sexual debauchery. **Open** Sunday-Thursday 1300-0100. Friday-Saturday 1300-0200

Dirty Dicks

Warmoesstraat 86, 1012 JH Phone **627 8634**
Otherwise known as the Sleaze Pit, a title that is well deserved. Only for the ultra-hardcore leather-and-jeans fraternity – screaming queens will not even get to the door! Well known for its watersports party on the last Thursday of the month. **Open** Friday-Saturday 2200-0400. Last Thursday 2100-0200 **Price** €4.50 for watersports party

Doll's Place

Vinkenstraat 57, 1013 JM Phone **627 0790**
Not a gay bar per se, but a nice local Dutch bar with a well and truly mixed crowd. Drinking, socialising and dancing is the order of the day, which for those of you who have been on your backs all weekend will come as some sort of relief. **Open** Monday-Thursday 2100-0300. Friday-Saturday 2100-0400

Downtown

Reguliersdwarsstraat 31, 1017 BJ Phone **622 9958**
This is a small gay café-bar famous for its apple pie. If apples aren't to your liking then there's lots of other cheap food and snacks which you can tuck into whilst reading through the English magazines and newspapers. Downtown has a nice, cruisey sidewalk terrace open in the summer. **Open** Sunday-Thursday 1000-2100. Friday-Saturday 1000-2200

The Eagle

Warmoesstraat 90, 1012 JH Phone **626 8634**
The Eagle is famous for at least two things. The first is the monthly Fist Fucking (FF) party that takes place on the first Sunday of each month. The second, now that you know the first reason, is that it is one of only a couple of bars in Amsterdam where you have to ring the bell for admission. The FF party starts at 1500 and goes right through to 2100 – admission €11.50. At all other times in the week, the Eagle plays host to the leather brigade doing the rounds between all the gay venues and their customary darkrooms on this world famous strip. **Open** Sunday-Thursday 2200-0400. Friday-Saturday 2200-0500

The Gaiety

Amstel 14, 1017 AA Phone **624 4271**
A popular bar with the young at heart taking advantage of the beautifully cruisey terrace overlooking the Amstel. **Open** Sunday-Thursday 1600-0100. Friday-Saturday 1600-0200

Getto

Warmoesstraat 51, 1012 HW Phone **421 5151** Web **www.getto.nl**
Trendy and rather camp bar at the front, inexpensive candlelit restaurant at the back. Tuesday is for women only (Getto Girls) and has, along with the Sunday sessions, become increasingly popular with both local and tourist girls as one of the places to hook up. There's a DJ over the weekend providing a party atmosphere ready to set you up for a night on the town. Happy hour runs Wednesday onwards from 1700-1900 although this only applies to cocktails. **Open** Tuesday 1900-0100. Wednesday-

Saturday 1600-0100. Sunday 1600-0000

Habibi Ana

Lange Leidsedwarsstraat 4-6, 1017 NL Phone **620 1788**
A popular Arabian gay bar and restaurant which was the surprise hit of the gay scene in Amsterdam when it opened in 2001. It's definitely a change from the usual suspects in this city, aimed at gay men and women of Middle Eastern, North African and Turkish descent though obviously also attracting a multitude of their admirers. A regular DJ plays music from the Middle East – giving rise to belly-dancing routines from those young things without middle-age spread or more than a six-pack – Bollywood favourites and more than a smattering of commercial tunes. Well worth a trip to the Leidseplein area to sample the delights on offer here. **Open** Sunday-Thursday 1700-0100. Friday-Saturday 1700-0300

Havana

Reguliersdwarsstraat 17-19, 1017 BJ Phone **620 6788**
Elegant and sizable gay bar with club upstairs. One of the few places that doesn't specifically cater for the leather-and-rubber scene – more for the young (and young at heart) with a penchant for dressing up ready for a night on the town. **Open** Monday-Thursday 1600-0100. Friday 1600-0300. Saturday 1400-0300. Sunday 1400-0100 **Price** €2-4 (for entry to the club only)

The Krokodil Bar

Amstelstraat 34 1017 DA Phone **626 2243**
Another venue claiming to be one of the oldest bars in Amsterdam, though this is more likely to apply to the age of the majority of the cus-

tomers. Good place for a relaxing drink or a quiet read of the papers during the week. However, on Sunday it does tend to get a little busier with a more diverse crowd. **Open** Monday-Sunday 1600-0200

Lellebel

Ultrechtsestraat 4, 1017 VM Phone 427 5139 Web **www.lellebel.nl**
Close to Rembrandtplein, this is Amsterdam's most popular drag cabaret bar, with karaoke and other forms of entertainment thrown in for good measure, particularly over the weekend. One of the few places in the city where trannies and their admirers tend to hook up and enjoy the convivial atmosphere. Happy hour on Sunday, 2000-2200. **Open** Monday-Thursday 2100-0300. Friday-Saturday 2000-0400. Sunday 2000-0300

Mankind

Weteringstraat 60, 1017 SP Phone **638 4755**
Web **www.mankind.nl**
Frank and Jon, the Dutch and English partners, operate this gay-friendly café-bar by the slow-moving waters of the Lijnbaansgracht a couple of blocks away from the museum and antiques quarter. Good, wholesome and affordable meals on offer, particular the dish of the day for €7.60 (including tea or coffee). A good place to while away a summer's afternoon while deciding how to spend the coming evening – sex again, most probably (*sigh*). **Open** Monday-Saturday 1200-0000. Sunday closed

Montmartre

Halvemaansteeg 17, 1017 CR Phone **620 7622**
The bar with the wall paintings – and all the pushing and shoving during the evening that a body can take. This is another Amstel campy hot-spot for tourists and locals alike. Its decor from a bygone era, loud music and uber-friendly barstaff make this place quite an alternative, and pleasant, place to spend at least a few hours. **Open** Sunday-Thursday 1700-0100. Friday-Saturday 1600-0300

The Music Box

Paardenstraat 9, 1017 CX Phone **620 4110**
In the past, Paardenstraat was the rent-boy (hustler) capital of the city. Today, the rent-boy activities have been considerably reduced, although it still represents the bulk of the pay-for-sex society. If you do plan to visit Paardenstraat, only take out with you the absolute minimum amount of money (enough for a shag and a few beers) and certainly not your credit cards or wallet as it's better to be safe than sorry round these parts.

Infamous barmaid Ricky works here: she is known to be rather upfront, so if you have any questions to ask about the boys she's the person to ask. **Open** Tuesday-Thursday 2100-0300. Friday-Saturday 2100-0400. Sunday 2100-0300

Night Life

Paardenstraat 7, 1017 CX Phone **420 9246**
Another rent-boy bar on Paardenstraat with very much the same story as The Music Box. Open Monday-Thursday 2000-0300. Friday-Saturday 2000-0400. Sunday 1700-0300

The Otherside

Reguliersdwarsstraat 6, 1017 BM Phone **625 5141**
Known throughout the civilized gay world as *the* gay coffeeshop. However, I don't think many of the punters who come in here realise it and carry on regardless, probably thinking what a nice, friendly young man that was behind the counter. This is strictly a coffeeshop (ie. no booze) but the atmosphere is enjoyable – and with all that dope in the place, who needs booze anyway? Worth popping in for the experience, although do try out some of the other coffeeshops in the city. Space cake sometimes available at around €4 a slice. Cannabis around €5 a gram. **Open** Monday-Sunday 1000-0100

The Queen's Head

Zeedijk 20, 1012 AL Phone **420 2475** Web **www.queenshead.nl**
This is a popular English bar owned by drag queen Dusty and his partner Johan. There's a kitsch 'traditional Dutch' canal house interior, with a beautiful view of this major canal junction within the red-light district. On Monday, beer is a mere €1 per glass; on Tuesday Dusty hosts her famous bingo nights, and on every first Wednesday of the month is Sportswear Day. The Billy Dolls in the window will probably stop you in your tracks as you pass by outside, and if you're a fan, Dusty and Johan will he happy to show you the rest of the collection once you're inside. The occassional theme nights, such as 'Worst Drag Queen', are popular. **Open** Monday-Thursday 1700-0100. Friday 1700-0300. Saturday 1600-0300. Sunday 1600-0100

Reality

Reguliersdwarsstraat 129, 1017 BL Phone **639 3012**
A hangout for black and Surinamese men, their friends and their admirers, and a very hospitable and friendly bar. **Open** Sunday-Thursday 2000-0300. Friday-Saturday 2000-0400

Saarein II

Elandsstraat 119, 1016 RX Phone **623 4901**
Saarein II used to be known as Saarein Bar, the sole women-only bar in Amsterdam, but, under new ownership, it recently started admitting men. Even so, this is still *the* bar for the fairer sex to come and meet. Saarein's long history resonates from its beautiful interior, much of which dates back to the seventeenth century. Having started off life as a political café back in the late seventies, these days Saarein is a cosy bar that is warm and friendly, replete with resident cat. It is split into three levels, including a bar, pool table and reading section. Events throughout the year worth mentioning are the Saarein birthday party, every third Sunday in August, and a contest for local weed growers which comes around on the last Friday of November. **Open** Sunday-Thursday 2000-0100. Friday-Saturday 2000-0200

Le Shako

Gravelandseveer 2, 1011 KM Phone **624 0209**
Opposite Amstel Taveerne. A totally unpretentious bar whose clientele ranges from locals and sex tourists to the (allegedly) drugged-up squatter, all crammed together to enjoy the cheap beer (even cheaper on a Tuesday) and the free munchies on a Thursday. **Open** Sunday-Thursday 2200-0300. Friday-Saturday 2200-0400

Showtime Bar

Halvemaansteeg 10, 1017 RD Phone **620 0171**
As the name suggests, the Showtime Bar tries to offer its clientele something a little bit different from the norm, from recitals to avant-garde cabaret evenings. It largely succeeds. It all takes place in a friendly and relaxing atmosphere. **Open** Sunday-Thursday 1400-0100. Friday-Saturday 1400-0200

Soho

Reguliersdwarsstraat 36, 1017 BM Phone **330 4400**
One of the most recent additions to the Amsterdam gay scene, this British- and American-style pub/bar arranged on two floors now seems to be firmly established as the place to be, ousting the former number-one hang-out, April, across the road. It has begun to be frequented by a few young rent boys – not a bad thing in itself, unless they become intimidating, but something you should be aware of. At midnight Soho offers two drinks for the price of one, thus guaranteeing that the place will be full come the witching hour. **Open** Sunday-Thursday 2000-0300. Friday-Saturday 2000-0400

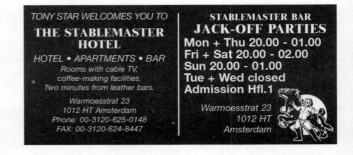

Spijker Bar

Kerkstraat 4, 1017 GL Phone **620 5919**
A more homely leather-and-jeans bar that's a lot less hardcore than the ones on and around Warmoesstraat. Most of the punters make use of the less intimidating darkroom facilities in the upstairs part of this small and intimate bar. Located on the other side of Kerkstraat to Thermos Night it can provide you with a little Dutch courage prior to a night of steamy sex. Depending on how drunk the punters are, the pool table at the back of the bar can, and usually does, double up as a shagging couch during the evening. **Open** Sunday-Thursday 1300-0200. Friday-Saturday 1300-0300

Stablemaster Bar

Warmoesstraat 23, 1012 HT Phone **624 5573**
A small leather/country and Western-style bar attached to the famous Stablemaster Hotel (see 'Accommodation listings'), renowned for its equally (in)famous JO (Jack Off/Wank) and safe-sex parties over the weekends. Leave your clothes at the door, pay your nominal admission of around €4.50, and enter into the dark and debaucherous interior. Condoms are naturally available free of charge and any attempts at unsafe sex will definitely be frowned upon. **Open** Thursday 2000-0100. Friday-Saturday 2000-0200. Sunday-Monday 2000-0100. Closed on Tuesday and Wednesday

Vandenberg

Lindengracht 95, 1017 BM Phone **622 2716**
A small bar/restaurant particularly popular with local lesbians and gays looking for a quiet evening out in the Jordaan part of the city. Better than average vegetarian menu with meals starting at around €12. **Open** Sunday-Thursday 1700-0100. Friday-Saturday 1000-0300

Vivelavie

Amstelstraat 7, 1017 DA Phone **624 0114**
This is a popular bar amongst lesbians who like to let their hair down. There's a mixed crowd of women in their 20s and 30s, but the music policy can, rather gratingly, veer towards a slightly more juvenile sound. Still, if you can put up with the trashy pap being churned out by the DJs, you'll be mixing with a young, up-for-it crowd. Ups and downs but the clientele make it worth a visit. **Open** Monday-Thursday 1500-0100 Friday-Saturday 1500-0300 Sunday 1500-0100

The Web

St Jacobusstraat 4-6, 1012 NC Phone **623 6758**
Leather-and-jeans bar that gets very busy early in the evening throughout the week, particularly on a Sunday. Usually the starting point for a 'leather' night on the town where the next stop would be the Cuckoo's Nest more or less around the corner. The upstairs darkroom sees a lot of the early action prior to the punters hitting the Warmoesstraat. Men only. **Open** Sunday-Thursday 1400-0100. Friday-Saturday 1400-0300

Why Not Bar and Blue Boy Club

Nieuwezijds Voorburgwal 28, 1012 RZ Phone **627 4374**
E-mail **info@whynot.nl** Web **www.whynot.nl**
The Why Not Bar and the Blue Boy Club are the same establishment with entrances on both Nieuwezijds Voorburgwal (Why Not) and Spuistraat 3 (Blue Boy). Both venues are connected to each other by a

stairway in the middle of the building. Why Not is a traditional bar on the ground floor where you can just pop in for a drink and enjoy the live sex shows performed on Thursday, Friday and Saturday at 2200. Tickets for these shows are €23. Included in this price is admission to the 20-odd seat porno cinema. You can buy your ticket at any time during the day and use the cinema as soon as you like. There is also a free strip show on the same days (from 2300) in the Blue Boy Club. It may be free but tipping is encouraged and you are required to purchase a drink. If you just want to view the porno movies in the cinema this will set you back about €6 for the entire day. For a one-hour escort in one of their rooms you can expect to pay in the region of €125 per hour in a standard room or €180 per hour in the well equipped S&M room or Thai Massage room. For hotel visits the price is around €130 per hour rising to €775 for a full 24 hours. The staff and boys at the Blue Boy (and Why Not) do have a well-established reputation for being friendly and non-intimidating. If you have never been to a House of Boys before, and want to, then you can pop in and view the photo album and discuss your requirements over a drink without feeling obliged in any way. **Open** Sunday-Thursday 1200-0100. Friday-Saturday 1200-0200

You II

Amstel 178 Phone **421 0900**
A couple of years old, You II came onto the scene as a welcome relief to lesbians, desperate for a new place to parade their wares. It pulls a similar crowd to the one that frequents Vivelavie earlier in the night, but its music policy (largely chart music) rather lets it down. Still, no woman

should leave Amsterdam without having experienced the club's standing toilet, or lady-pee as it's called (I have it on good information that it's well-worth the excursion). **Open** Daily, late

Clubs and club nights

COC Amsterdam

Rozenstraat 14, 1016 NX Phone **626 3087** Web **www.cocamsterdam.nl**
COC is the city's gay rights and information centre located on a side street off the Prinsengracht. It holds and organises regular party nights and events for many of the city's gay groups. On Friday their upstairs disco is very well attended, as much by locals as by tourists, and the atmosphere is positively convivial. The music on Friday starts off with eurotrashy pop and slowly, as the night progresses, gets slightly more house-oriented although sticking to the more vocal style. Saturday is the long, long running women-only night which gets rather busy, due to the fact that – surprisingly – there is not much in the city for women (well, not compared with what the men have got). During the day the small café on the ground floor of the building gets a good crowd in for coffee and snacks and to find out the latest happenings in the city. Maps, leaflets and magazines are available in the lobby. **Open** (Club) Friday-Saturday 2300-0400. (Café) Tuesday-Thursday 1000-0000. Friday-Saturday 1000-0400. Sunday 1000-0000 **Price €4** (Friday and Saturday)

Cockring

Warmoesstraat 96, 1012 JH Phone **623 9604** Web **www.clubcockring.com**
If you can't get sex in here (as opposed to not wanting sex in here – eh?) then you must be the ugliest person on the planet. Two floors of high energy, men-only sexual tension – very popular, very sweaty, very hot – in fact it is the premier gay leather-and-seedy-sex-club in the city for the leather-and-jeans set. The darkroom is obviously the main draw of this place, however the dance arena with its hard-house vibe provides welcome relief from the shady goings-on in the other parts of the club. Hot, live sex shows are provided every Thursday and Sunday at 2300, and underwear parties every first Wednesday of the month – check at the club for alternating dates. There is usually no door charge but the drinks are expensive. In addition to the normal club nights the Cockring hosts special sex parties on the first and third Sunday of the month. Every first

Sunday is Nude Club – strict dress code of shoes or boots only. Every third Sunday is Horsemen and Knights – a naked, partially naked or underwear-only dress code in force for those who are hung like horses (horsemen) and their admirers (the knights). My guess is that there are always more knights than horsemen – like I say, just a guess! If you are interested, get here early. Doors open at 1500 and the party begins at 1600, attracting 80 to 100-plus people and going on until 1900. The atmosphere is spirited, you can do as much or as little as you want, so if you are inclined just to sit at the bar and watch then that is totally acceptable. If, however, getting up and shaking your bits and booty to all and sundry is your thing, then the ones who are sitting at the bar will be a more than appreciative audience. Come 1730, free sandwiches are served (Have you washed your hands?). **Open** Sunday-Thursday 2300-0400. Friday-Saturday 2300-0500 **Price** €6.50 for special events, otherwise free

Coco Latté @ The Back Door

Amstelstraat 32, 1017 DA Phone **620 2333**
Web **www.backdoor.nl** and **www.cocolatte.net**
A household name on the London club scene, Coco Latté opened their monthly residency in Amsterdam at the Back Door during Easter 2002. Their mixed gay and gay-friendly party night has transferred well and the hard, cutting-edge house music provided by long-term resident DJs Mark Bambach and Luigi Rosi will no doubt establish this event as the one not to be missed. **Open** Last Friday of the month 2300-0500 **Price** €12

Exit

Reguliersdwarsstraat 42, 1017 BJ Phone **625 8788**
One of the most popular bar and club set-ups in this notoriously gay area. Its main clientele is the young, tight white T-shirt and muscles brigade but the bar does seem to attract a diverse crowd including a lesbian contingent. Music in the club is a mix of commercial chart gravitating, as the evening wears on, to a harder vocal house vibe. The darkroom upstairs is popular and well used by the lads on the pull and definitely not as heavy as the playrooms in the leather districts. **Open** Sunday-Thursday 2300-0400. Friday-Saturday 2300-0500 **Price** €6-8 Friday-Saturday

Heat @ The Back Door

Amstelstraat 32, 1017 DA Phone **620 2333** Web **www.backdoor.nl**
Another gay, straight-friendly night at this swish venue. Hard pumping hands in the air, shirts on the floor, house music happening . . . the trouble is you have to decide which venue will be the best, either here or the

Your Gay Way to Amsterdam

Subscribe online!
www.gay-news.com

The monthly gay magazine in both English and Dutch. Guiding since 1992, now the largest bilingual gay publication in the country. With all the latest information, the latest updates of the Gay Map, parties, extensive agenda's, background-info and much more. Available in the better bookshops for € 3.15 Gay News, completing your Amsterdam visit

For inquiries please
dial (+31) 020- 679 15 56
fax (+31) 020- 670 14 70
or email info@gaynews.nl

10th
Anniversary

BOYSNETWORK

.co.uk
.com
.nl
.be
.net

Let's meet

gay news

gay

gayamsterdam.com
straight to the source

© photo:Jay EH

Party updates,
hotel bookings,
upcoming events, contacts,
NEW dating system,
instant messaging,
xrated material and movies,
extensive shop, agenda's,
chat, Amsterdam picture and
nightlife archives:
turn directly to the source! Turn
to our monthly Gay News, or
visit our fully interactive
websites, consisting over 14
integrated sites,
main gateway
www.gayamsterdam.com

gay night at More... hmm, the decisions you have to make when you are gay and in Amsterdam. See also the 'Club and club night' listings for Coco Latté and the Sunday Tea Dance. **Open** Wednesday 2300-0400 **Price** €5

iT

Amstelstraat 24, 1017 DA Phone **421 6924** Web **www.it.nl**
Infamous and long-running, strictly gay disco night going by the name Gay Gang Bang. Thumping house music progressively gets harder through the evening, pleasing the hedonistic sea of nearly naked flesh on the massive dancefloor.Be prepared to have your sexuality questioned if you do not look gay (!) and be prepared to be refused entry. Prince – the artist formerly known as barmy – has been refused entry in the past and it added to the kudos of the place. Straight nights on Thursday-Friday 2300-0400 also have their fair share of gay attendance and can make for an equally good night out. For those on a tight budget, it's worth knowing that the drinks' prices in here border on the extortionate – pills or pop, you decide! It is customary to tip the doormen on the way out but if you had to bear the brunt of their attitude on the way in then you can politely ask them to kiss your arse! **Open** Saturday 2300-0500 **Price** €7-9.50

Pussy Lounge @ Melkweg

Lijnbaansgracht 234A,1017 PH Phone **531 8181** (**Melkweg**)
E-mail **reception@melkweg.nl** Web **www.melkweg.nl**
Formerly at Roxy, Pussy Lounge has now moved to the Old Hall in the amazing De Melkweg complex. It's a women-only event that comes around but once a month, featuring some of the best dance music

around, courtesy of **DJ Natarcia**, among others. Dates are announced in advance in the local gay papers, so keep you eyes peeled and don't miss out on one of Amsterdam's most successful and enjoyable nights out for the ladies. **Open** 2200-0100 **Price** €10

S.O.S. Sex on Sunday @ Argos

Warmoesstraat 95, 1012 HZ Phone **622 6595**
E-mail **leather@argosbar.demon.nl**
Long-running and well-documented Sunday men-only sex party (nude and semi-nude). **Open** Last Sunday of the month 1500-0200 (doors close at 1600 – be early if you want to get in) **Price** €5

Tea Dance @ The Back Door

Amstelstraat 32, 1017 DA Phone **620 2333** Web **www.backdoor.nl**
Well-established Sunday gay foray in this trendy and welcoming club. Complimentary food, joints, cigs (do they really think we can be swayed with the promise of free joints?). Uplifting vocal house. See also the club night listings for Coco Latté and Heat. **Open** Sunday 2100-0400 **Price** €9

Club Trash

Oostelijke Handelskade 21 Phone **639 2335**
Sex party every third Saturday of the month in the eastern part of Amsterdam. Private cabins, sling room, watersports room, bondage room, two additional darkrooms, chill-out area, condoms and gloves, buzzin' dancefloor with Amsterdam's best DJs. Strict dress code of rubber, leather and fetish – but no jeans! Always get the current details from COC, RoB (usual sponsors) or any of the other gay leather/sex shops listed as the venue changes often. Also, you are well advised to check whether there is a minibus or coach going to the event – there often is. The annual Megatrash weekend, a party that stretches over 14 solid, sleazy, sexy hours, usually takes place in August. Tickets (around €30) for this event sell out early so book well ahead. **Open** Third Saturday of the month 2300-0700 **Price** €12-15

De Trut

Bilderdijkstraat 165, 1053 KP Phone **612 3524**
Hard-house and trance dance club with full gay-only door policy. A bit out of the way but well worth going to the trouble to find. The entrance is unmarked but if you turn up between 2300 and midnight you'll soon see where to go. The club fills up early and more often than not you will have to adhere to their strict one out/one in door policy. The music is regarded as the best in any of the Amsterdam clubs and yet the organis-

ers consistently work this place on a not-for-profit basis. The drinks are cheap and so are the punters – so the pick-up potential is quite high. **Open** Sunday 2300-0400

Village @ More

Rozengracht 133 1016 LV Web **www.expectmore.nl**
With a capacity of 750-plus, More is one of the 'superclubs' of the city. Opening its trendy doors back in 2000, it has become one of the places where it is cool to be seen. The week starts off with a 'gay night' called Village, their adverts proclaiming that this is where all subsections of the gay community can get together for a night of US garage with the odd set of disco (eek), R&B and house (hard and commercial). The cynical ones amongst us would proclaim that we are easy money on a normally quiet night. Friday is Glamore – 2300-0400 (€11) – for the majority straight crowd who like to dress up and show off. Visiting DJs from around the world are the pull and pull the crowds they do. If music more than sex is your bag, then this night in Amsterdam will not be wasted. Saturday is Club Risk – 2300-0500 (€12) – when a young fashionable crowd enjoy house music of the most serious order. Should you not be deemed cool enough to enter these hallowed portals, tell the bouncers where to stick it and make your way across the road to the less selective Mazzo (Rozengracht 114) where the music is just as good (house-wise) and the bouncers not such arseholes! Its not gay though – but in Amsterdam who really cares? **Open** Wednesday 2300-0500 **Price** €7

Saunas

Boomerang

Heintje Hoeksteeg 8, 1012 GR Phone **622 6162**
The sauna is very easy to find down a small side street off Warmoesstraat. It's a lot smaller than the two Thermos venues and the vibe throughout is noticeably friendlier, particularly from the staff who take the time to talk to you and explain where everything is. Due to it being in the red-light district, you tend to get more bisexual and closeted married men here than in Thermos, which for some people is a turn-on in itself. All the regular facilities are to hand – sauna cabin, Jacuzzi, steam room and the all-important darkrooms – however, due to space limitations around this area, they are small and certainly not exceptional. Well worth spending a couple of hours in here when you are feeling a

little bit randy. **Open** Monday-Sunday 0900-2300 **Price** €11.19 or €8.95 for students and under-24s

Thermos Day

Raamstraat 33, 1016 XL Phone **623 4936** Web **www.thermos.nl**
Thermos Day, sister venue to Thermos Night, is located on a quiet side street off Prinsengracht. The usual facilities are spread out over five floors of prime real estate including a beauty salon (accessible from the street as well as from inside the sauna) and a bar. As you would expect, and similar to Thermos Night, the bulk of the space is given over to the darkrooms, mazes of corridors and playrooms. The place always seems to be busy and the fun comes in just wandering around looking for the perfect partner (of which there are many) or diving in at the deep end and joining the swathes of naked flesh in the steam room or sauna. Surprisingly there is no pressure here – you are left to your own devices and the usual bitchiness and cliques found in many similar establishments just does not exist. The lighting in many of the areas could be slightly enhanced but that is just a small niggle in what is an excellent venue. **Open** Monday-Friday 1200-2300. Saturday 1200-2200. Sunday 1100-2200 **Price** €17.50. Under-24s €12.50

Thermos Night

Kerkstraat 58-60, 1017 GM Phone **623 4936** Web **www.thermos.nl**
From 0200, this place gets packed, particularly at the weekend when the upstairs floor containing all the cabins is the place to head for. There's little doubt that you will see someone who takes your fancy, but finding an unoccupied cabin can at times become rather frustrat-

ing. Like the day sauna, the atmosphere is convivial and relaxed, probably because many of the punters have had a drink or two, which does help to remove inhibitions (and get them a bit randy!). Another must visit! **Open** Sunday-Friday 2300-0800. Saturday 2300-1000 **Price** €17.50. Under-24s €12.50

Mandate Gay Gym

Prinsengracht 715, 1017 JW Phone **625 4100**
Men-only gymnasium with the addition of a small sauna and solarium. **Open** Monday-Friday 1100-2200. Saturday 1200-1800. Sunday 1400-1800 **Price** Guest admission €9

Accommodation

Accommodation Outlet

32 Old Compton Street, Soho, London W1D 4TP England
Phone **+00 44 (0)20 7287 4244** Fax **+00 44 (0)20 7734 7217**
E-mail **holidays@outlet.co.uk** Web **www.outlet4holidays.com**
Outlet has a variety of holiday accommodation available for visitors to Amsterdam, from a private studio apartment for two people, to a houseboat for five. Since 1995, Accommodation Outlet has been offering the largest selection of low-cost, self-catering accommodation in London. It has now expanded its horizons to Europe, and Amsterdam. Cleanliness, good service, excellent location, double- or king-sized beds, cable TV, cotton linen, towels, and compact disc music systems are standard with most of Outlet's accommodation. A comprehensive and interactive website is being updated regularly with extensive descriptions of all their properties, complete with colour photographs taken from within the apartments and maps to enable you to see exactly where your property is located. There's a currency converter too to help you work out the cost of your accommodation before booking. You can make your reservation either on-line, at the office or by phone. Outlet's London headquarters acts as a valuable resource centre offering both lesbian and gay tourist advice and information – feel free to contact them with queries about their services. Travellers can also look forward to the end of this year and next as Outlet set about launching similar services in Barcelona, Sitges, Paris, Berlin, New York, Sydney and San Francisco. **Open** Monday-Friday 1000-1900. Saturday 1200-1700 **Prices** from €85

Aero Hotel

Kerkstraat 49, 1017 GB Phone **622 7728**
Small, gay hotel in the middle of one of Amsterdam's most famous gay streets. Rooms are clean and comfortable but nothing special. The hotel takes in four floors and if you are in one of the top rooms you have an amazing number of stairs to climb. If you have a plastic hip or powdery bones then I recommend you ask for a room on the first or second floor. **Price** €50-80 double

Amistad Hotel

Kerkstraat 42, 1017 GM Phone **624 8074**
E-mail **info@amistad.nl** Web **www.amistad.nl**
Formerly known as the Westend, this newly renovated gay hotel is above the late-opening Cosmo Bar. It is one of the oldest gay hotels in Amsterdam, offering comfortable new rooms and a communal and friendly breakfast room. All rooms have private or shared bathrooms, telephone, personal safe, fridge and colour TV, and guests are provided with their own front-door key. On Wednesday you can join everyone else for a 'dinner among friends' before hitting the clubs. **Price** €60-95 single; €72-120 double; €30 per extra bed

Amsterdam Connection

Lijnbaansgracht 252, 1017 RK Phone **625 7412**
Furnished self-catering apartments equipped with private facilities, TV and kitchenette. **Price** from €50

Amsterdam Holiday Apartment

Korsjespoortsteeg Phone **261 361** or (UK) **+ 00 44 (0)7989 412456**
E-mail **amsterdam.apartment@btopenworld.com**
Web **http:/amsterdam.apartment.users.btopenworld.com**
Furnished private studio-apartment for two in the historic central canal neighbourhood. Equipped with cable TV, stereo, en-suite facilities and fully equipped kitchen. You will get the address when you book – it's only a ten-minute walk from Centraal Station and the scene. **Price** On request

Amsterdam House

Amstel 176A, 1017 AE Phone **626 2577** E-mail **amshouse@euronet.nl**
Apartments and houseboats to let for short or long stays. Close to the Centraal Station and other major transport intersections. In total there are over 30 apartments and six houseboats to let. All are spacious and fully furnished, some with sauna and Jacuzzi. **Price** from €57 single; €102 double; €135 triple; €300 three-bedroomed houseboat

Anco Hote

Oudezijds Voorburgwal 55, 1012 EJ Phone **624 1126**
E-mail **info@ancohotel.nl** Web **www.ancohotel.nl**
Located opposite the Oude Kerk (Old Church) by the canal behind Warmoesstraat, this popular men-only hotel caters for leathermen and their admirers. All the rooms have cable TV with a non-stop gay video channel. Early bookings are advised. Rates include continental breakfast, served between 0900 and 1130 at the bar. **Price** €52 single; €75 double; €34 dorms; €110 studios

Barangay Bed & Breakfast

Droogbak 15, 1013 GG Phone **504 5432**
E-mail **barangay@chello.nl** Web **www.barangay.nl**
This is the charming guest-house of Wimmo and Godwin, built in 1777 on Amsterdam's former coastline, complete with original façade, and close to the Jordaan area of Amsterdam. Droogbak itself is a lovely, quiet area – amazing given that it is only one street away from the longest shopping street in the Netherlands. Most of the tourist attractions are, subsequently, well within easy walking distance. Note that this is a strictly no-smoking establishment. **Price** €80-125

Black Tulip

Geldersekade 16, 1012 BH Phone **427 0933** Fax **624 4281**
Web **www.blacktulip.nl**
The Black Tulip is an exclusively gay hotel on the edge of the Warmoesstraat leather district, a couple of minutes from Centraal Station. All rooms in this upmarket and stylish 16th-century canalside building come with private bathroom, TV/VCR, telephone, safe deposit box, minibar and tea/coffee-making facilities. Rooms are 'tastefully' furnished with a sling and bondage hooks as standard, plus additional pieces such as St Andrew's cross, bondage chair, stocks and metal cages (you can view the rooms on their website). Items that you may have forgotten to bring can also be rented at the hotel – such as boots, suspension sets, sleepsacks (excluding hoods) and so forth. Price from €105 single to €175 Black Fantasy room, inclusive of breakfast buffet

Cage Guesthouse

Address on application Phone **420 5656** E-mail **cage1@planet.nl**
Web **www.cage-amsterdam.nl**
A double-roomed apartment opposite Centraal Station, two minutes away from the leather bars on Warmoesstraat and even closer to the Queen's Head. Separate entrance with your own key, en-suite bathroom

with Jacuzzi, tea/coffee-making facilities, fridge and cable TV with the added bonus of a metal cage to play with! **Price** €70 per night

Centre Apartments Amsterdam

Heintje Hoekssteeg, 1012 GR Phone **627 2503**
E-mail **caa-gd@wxs.nl** Web **www.gay-apartments-amsterdam.nl**
Fully-fitted, self-catering apartments and studios, about 15 in all, situated in a small street off Warmoesstraat. Clean and comfortable rooms these certainly are, however, the firm, but fair, rules of the house may be a bit off-putting to some people. **Price** from €112 (studios for one or two people) to €135 (apartment for one to three people sharing). Foldaway beds €40 extra

Chico's Guesthouse

St Willibordusstraat 77, 1073 VA Phone **675 4241**
Small private guest-house with three guest rooms and two private apartments. **Price** €43-55

The Collector Bed & Breakfast

De Lairessestraat 46, 1071 PB Phone **673 6779**
E-mail **karel@the-collector.nl** Web **www.the-collector.nl**
This unusual bed and breakfast can be found just behind the Concertgebouw, a five-minute walk from the Rijksmuseum, the Van Gogh Museum and the Stedelijk Museum, and within easy walking distance of the city centre. As the name of the place suggests, the well-appointed rooms in this large house dating back to 1914 are filled with 'collections' inspired by the art deco period. **Price** €80-102 single; €90-114 double; €102-125 triple; breakfast included

Drake's Guest House

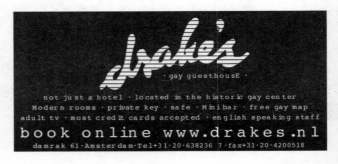

Damrak 61, 1012 LM Phone **638 2367**
E-mail **drakes@drakes.nl** Web **www.drakes.nl**
Gay-owned Drake's has three guest-houses in the city centre, providing twelve rooms in all, each with a double bed, shower and toilet, mini-bar and colour TV (with their own in-house gay video channel). The houses at Damrak 61 and Nieuwendijk 20 are near to the Queen's Palace and only two blocks away from the Warmoesstraat, Europe's leather capital, while the house at Keizersgracht 669 is in a canalside location close to Rembrandtplein. From each house it's only a short walk or tram ride to most of the gay bars, discos and nightlife. Guests receive a complimentary ticket to Drake's Sex Cinema, the cruisiest cinema in Amsterdam (see 'Retail and other listings'). **Price** from €85-

200 per room

E and D City Apartments

Singel 34, 1015 AA Phone **624 7335** E-mail **nicenew@worldonline.nl**
Apartments for one or two people in the Jordaan area of the city. Minimum stay of three nights required. Usually caters for leather-and-jeans gays. **Price** from €98

Escape Apartments

Web **www.amsterdamescape.com**
A selection of apartments in central Amsterdam, ideal for groups of six to 21 people wanting to share an entire house. Very stylish and far better than sharing different rooms in a hotel. Website allows you to view the apartments, check availability and to book direct. **Price** from €60 per person sharing, based on a group of twelve or more

Flatmates Amsterdam

Java Island Phone **6201545**
E-mail **info@flatmates.nl** Web **www.flatmates.nl**
Exclusively gay acommodation sitauted on Java Island, which is a five-minute boat ride from Centraal Station, or a 15-minute walk over the bridge that spans the Het Ij. Your hosts, Hans and Rui, pride themselves on providing the gay community with the best standards of accommodation they can. The modern, clean rooms come with awesome waterside views, a small kitchenette and cable TV. Ask also about their apartment in Egelantiersgracht, in the Jordaan. **Price** From €85 for a single room per night, and €115 per double room per night

Frederick Park House

Frederiksplein 22, 1017 XM Phone **420 7726**
E-mail **frederik.park.house@wxs.nl**
A small, well-presented and friendly guest-house-cum-hotel situated in a quiet part of old Amsterdam and facing the park. It's close to all of the facilities and attractions of the old city and beyond, with good access to public transport. Just around the corner from here you can unearth a wide variety of restaurants, shops and traditional Amsterdam bars. **Price** from €90 double to €175 three-person apartment

Freeland Hotel

Marnixstraat 36, 1017 PL Phone **622 7511**
A mixed gay and straight budget hotel with better than average facilities and handy for Jordaan and the Leidseplein. All 15 rooms have en-suite facilities, TV and telephone and they even include a full Dutch break-

fast. **Price** from €65

Golden Bear

Kerkstraat 37, 1017 GB Phone 624 4785
E-mail **info@goldenbear.nl** Web **www.goldenbear.nl**
Founded in the 1940s, the Golden Bear claims to be Amsterdam's first gay hotel. The rooms are comfortable, with either full en-suite or shared facilities, and all single rooms have double beds. Breakfast is available until 1200, quite a bonus as the hotel is on the same strip as Thermos Night and you may need the odd lie-in! The Bear is a very, very popular choice and it's best to book way in advance. **Price** from €53 single; €79 standard twin; €107 de-luxe twin

Greenhouse Effect Hotel

Warmoesstraat 53-55, 1012 HW Phone 624 4974
E-mail **stay@greenhouse-effect.nl** Web **www.greenhouse-effect.nl**
Not a gay hotel but as it's on one of the gayest streets in Amsterdam's red-light district it's a good place to be based. The hotel is located above the famous Greenhouse Effect coffee shop and bar, where guests can enjoy breakfast until 1200 and happy-hour prices on pints of beer and cider all day. There's also a cocktail to savour that goes by the name of 'Cream In Your Pants'. Well, I don't mind if I do. There are no curfew restrictions, so coming and going as you like is not a problem. The GHE Bar is well known for its modern dance and electronic music and with nightly DJs and a party atmosphere the place is a hedonist's delight – if you want quiet, look elsewhere. Accommodation standards are high in the nine rooms. **Price** from €50 standard single; €75 standard twin; €85-110 en-suite twin

Hotel Greenwich Village

Kerkstraat 25, Amsterdam 1017 GB Phone 626 9746
Clean, comfortable and affordable mainly gay hotel close to Spijker Bar and Thermos Night. Rooms sleeping five people are also available. Expect to have to leave a refundable key deposit. Very friendly. **Price** from €85 per night

ITC Hotel

Prinsengracht 1051, 1017 JE Phone 623 0230
E-mail **office@itc-hotel.com** Web **www.itc-hotel.com**
The International Travel Club Hotel is a large, authentic canal house overlooking a quiet stretch of Amsterdam's grandest canal. It's one of the prettiest gay hotels in Amsterdam, located in a quite neighbourhood

yet right in the heart of the city, under ten minutes' walk from the main gay areas, Kerkstraat and Rembrandplein – no surpise therefore that you should book well in advance. There are 20 charming rooms, all rooms come complete with TV, telephone and private safe, and a breakfast buffet is served until 1200 each day. Popular with the older crowd for what difference that makes. **Price** €55-65 single; €75-115 double; €130 triple

Jordaan Canal House

Eglantiersgracht 23, 1015RC Phone **620 1545**
E-mail **hanspluygers@csi.com**
An enchanting seventeenth-century canal house that is exclusively gay, excellently appointed and in a quiet location – simply unique! From its central position in the historic quarter of the Jordaan known as 'The Garden of Amsterdam' it is a short, pleasant walk to the gay district and to most visitor attractions. **Price** from €90

Krasnapolsky Apartments

Oudezijds Voorburgwal, Dam 9, 1012 JS Phone **554 9111**
E-mail **info@krasnapolsy.nl** Web **www.krasnapolsky.nl**
Not gay, but these luxurious apartments (part of the Krasnapolsky Hotel, where you should check in) reside in restored listed buildings just behind Dam Square in amongst the heart of it all. Each of the 36 apartments has its own private entrance and is fully furnished, combining first-class living accommodation with all the facilities you would expect from a five-star hotel. Rates are inclusive of VAT and housekeeping service once a week, but exclude a 5-per-cent city tax. There is a €10 discount per night for a minimum stay of 30 nights (the minimum stay here is two weeks). The Junior apartments (for a maximum of two people) come with one bedroom, living room, luxury kitchen (with microwave and dishwasher) and bathroom (with bath and/or shower and toilet). The Business apartments (for a maximum of two people) also have one bedroom, and are similar to the Junior apartments, but are more spacious and luxurious. Most apartments offer a view over the canal, and some Business apartments have a view over the inner garden. The De Luxe apartments (for a maximum of four people) have one bedroom, and are similar to the Business apartments, but with extra beds and a loft over the bedroom. Finally, there are the Superior De Luxe apartments (for a maximum of four people), which come with two bedrooms, a spacious living room and a big, luxury kitchen (with microwave). The Superior apartments have a view out over the canal. **Price** Junior €110; Business €145; De Luxe €160; Superior De Luxe €230

Krasnapolsky Hotel

Dam 9, 1012 JS Phone **554 9111**
E-mail **info@krasnapolsky.nl** Web **www.krasnapolsky.nl**
The luxury five-star Golden Tulip Grand Hotel Krasnapolsky is located in the very heart of Amsterdam on Dam Square, opposite the Royal Palace, and is surrounded by department stores, boutiques and shopping alleys. There are 468 rooms, several bars and restaurants, a beauty salon and fitness room, and a conference centre. All the rooms are superbly equipped with free tea/coffee-making facilities, hairdryer, safe, air conditioning, IDD telephone, mini-bar, trouser press and cable TV with an in-house film channel. Rates are per room per night, excluding

breakfast (€20) and city tax (5%). **Price** from €115 standard single/double; €310 executive/royal view; €710 suite with a roof terrace.

Maes Bed and Breakfast

Herenstraat 26, 1015 CB Phone **427 5165**
E-mail **maesbb94@xs4all.nl** Web **www.xs4all.nl/~maesbb94**
A strictly no-smoking guesthouse named after seventeenth-century Dutch painter Nicolaas Maes, a pupil of Rembrandt. Located in a quiet street between the Herengracht and Keizersgracht, it is only a few steps away from the Anne Frank House and the shops, restaurants and galleries of the Jordaan. The Rijksmuseum and the Van Gogh and Stedelijk museums are also within walking distance. The rooms in this recently renovated eighteenth-century house are comfortable, prices include an extended continental breakfast, and there's a guest kitchen on the first floor. **Price** €70-90 (single) €84-130 (double) €114-130 (apartment)

Hotel De Mallemoolen

Warmoesstraat 7, 1012 HT Phone **535 3222**
De Mallemoolen isn't a gay hotel but it is well located in a gayer-than-gay area on the Warmoesstraat. This is a hotel that will suit those on a tight budget, who will have the choice of 13 affordable, well-presnted rooms that vary from single to quad accommodation. Next door is the Hotel De Koopermoolen, where the reception (with internet facilities) is located and where a full breakfast buffet is served. Centraal Station is barely five minutes away and there are bars, restaurants and shops very close. **Price** from €70 single; €115 double; €235 triple; €235 quad; €60 extra bed. Suite available at the Hotel De Koopermoolen (next door) for €200

Hotel Orfeo

Leidsekruisstraat 14, 1017 RH Phone **623 1347**
With 22 rooms, Orfeo is Amsterdam's largest exclusively gay hotel. Located in the centre of the city, it is within a short walk of the Leidseplein, the Kerkstraat and the Reguliersdwarsstraat's gay scenes. Also within a short walk are Amsterdam's major art museums. **Price** from €45 single; €61-66 double/twin

Hotel Orlando

Prinsengracht 1099, 1017 JH Phone **638 6915**
Hotel Orlando is a small, well-designed, five-room hotel in a pretty, converted seventeenth-century canal house. **Price** from €59-90 single; €73-125 double

Prinsen Hotel

Vondelstraat 36-38, 1054 GE Phone **616 2323**
Web **www.prinsenhotel.demon.nl**
This recently renovated 45-room hotel is centrally located close to the Leidseplein. It has the friendly atmosphere of a three-star hotel where personal attention and service are a matter of course. All rooms have a direct-dial telephone, TV, hairdryer and private safe. **Price** from €90 single; €115 double

Hotel Quentin

Leidsekade 89, 1017 PN Phone **626 2187**
The hotel is situated by the Singelgracht, in the heart of Amsterdam, just off the Leidseplein, close to all the gay bars, clubs and events. A friendly and small hotel, the rooms here, with or without private facilities, are ideal for the budget traveller. All rooms have cable TV and direct-dial telephone. **Price** €31-50 single; €50-108 double; €75-118 triple

Hotel Quentin England

Roemer Visscherstraat 30, 1054 EZ Phone **699 2323**
Three-star gay-friendly hotel located in a residential area close to the Leidseplein. **Price** €39-66 single; €50-80 double; €77-109 triple

Rubens Bed & Breakfast

Rubensstraat 38, 1077 MS Phone **662 9187**
E-mail **info@rubensbb.com** Web **www.rubensbb.com**
This no-smoking bed and breakfast is conveniently located in a 1930s residential neighbourhood in the city centre. The up-market shopping street Beethovenstraat is nearby and the major museums and tourist attractions are within walking distance or a few tram stops. One room is decorated in art deco style and has the option of a private bathroom, the other is decorated in traditional Friesian style, from the town of Hindeloopen. Both have double beds. **Price** €80-98 per room. Minimum stay of three nights

Hotel Sander

Jacob Obrechtstraat 69, 1071 KJ Phone **662 7574**
This three-star hotel has 20 pleasant and pristine en-suite rooms, each equipped with TV, phone and safe. This place is centrally located and very close to many of the city's main tourist attractions, and the friendly staff will be happy to give you information what to do when in Amsterdam. A traditional Dutch breakfast every morning should see you fit and raring to put their recommendations to the test. **Price** €66-85 single; €85-102 double; €118-145 triple

Stablemaster Hotel

Warmoesstraat 23, 1012 HT Phone **625 0148**
Situated above the Stablemaster Bar (see 'Bars listings'), and a two-minute stroll from the leather district. Apartments available from €90. Rooms come with cable TV and coffee-making facilities. **Price** from €85 (double)

Sunhead of 1617

Herengracht 152, 1016 BN Phone **626 1809**
E-mail **carlos@sunhead.com** Web **www.sunhead.com**
A charming 400-year-old canal house along Amsterdam's most beautiful canal, the Herengracht. It sits in a fabulous central location and offers spacious cosy rooms all with en-suite facilities, fridge, microwave, tea/coffee-making facilities and cable TV. **Price** €106-116

The Townhouse

Akoleienstraat 2, 1016 LN Phone **612 9320**
E-mail **info@townhouse.nl** Web **www.townhouse.nl**
Situated in the Jordaan, The Townhouse is a comfy bed and breakfast situated on the first floor of a nineteenth-century townhouse. You can afford a lie-in (breakfast is served until 1400!). Smartly presented rooms with cable TV, tea/coffee-making facilities, fridge and safe on request. There's even a nice touch of fresh flowers and fruit. Price €89

Vijaya Hotel

Oudezijds Voorburgwal 44, 1012 GE Phone **638 0102**
Vijaya is a two-star hotel (not gay) located right in the middle of Amsterdam, a three-minute walk from Centraal Station, Dam Square and the main shopping streets and 15 minutes from the Leidseplein and the Rembrandtplein. All the rooms have en-suite facilities, TV, radio and intercom. Breakfast is included in the room price. **Price** from €60 single; € 82 double; €115 triple; €135 quad

Hotel Winston

Warmoesstraat 123-129, 1012 JA Phone **623 1380** Web **www.winston.nl**
Not a gay hotel. The Winston, located in the heart of Amsterdam on the city's oldest street, is a 66-room hotel, with a bar, two clubs, and art – not just in frames, but eyeing you everywhere you turn. If you are looking for quaint, then move along, because the Winston is not tulips or lace curtains, but a pulsating, pounding place to stay, to hang, to be – a particular favourite with artists and those with an artistic bent. The hotel is 20 minutes from the airport, five minutes from the Centraal Station, and 2 minutes from the red-light district. **Price** €35-50 single; €45-65 double; €55-75 triple; €90 quad (breakfast extra)

Cruising grounds

The cruising scene in Amsterdam is small and you'll find nowhere near the diversity nor riches of a place like London. When you can easily pick up rent boys at the station or slip into any one of dozens of clubs, bars and saunas with darkrooms, the need for, and patronising of, such a scene is slim. Still, if you must get your willy out in the wild, then you could try the following known cruising areas.

The **Vondelpark** is perhaps the most renowned of them, with action taking place late at night at the Rosarium area, close to the Emmastraat entrance. Also famous and still popular is the **Nieuwe Meer** on the south side of the city, where nudity is fairly common and cruising takes place day and night. The particular area to aim for is close to the Mercure Hotel, although when the sun is out, the area starts to expand to accommodate its extra patrons. North-west of Centraal Station is **Westerpark**, and as night-time segues into the early hours of the morning, the area behind the Stadsdeel building starts to hot up, with action spreading across the bushes that line the watery trenches of the Haarlemmervaart.

Other possibilities could be the post-midnight hours at **Frederik Hendrik Plantsoen**, west of the Amstel, not far from the Heineken Brewery. If you're out of luck there, nip down Frederik Henderikstraat for a similarly late call-in at **Bilderdijkpark**, within piddling distance of the Hugo de Grootgracht. A quick rummage around here could spring a surprise or two. Whilst passing through the Pijp neighbourhood, it may be worth nipping into **Sarphatipark** and sniffing out some action in the south-west corner, away from the Amstel end. And if you're heading way out of the centre then the eastern end of **Julianapark**, close to Amstel Station, is rumoured to be busy both day and night. Still, if your hankering for a good outdoor seeing-to has still not been sated then your best bet could be lie far further afield. You need to head south out of the city for Zandvoort (a good half-hour drive away) and make your way to the gay nudist beach. The dunes there are not an official part of the nudist area, but, nonethless, you'll find heads bobbing up and down here like meerkats at an amphetamine-fuelled rave.

Of course, there's no place like your own doorstep, and if your hotel doorstep happens to be located centrally you could – cautiously – try one of the pissoirs in the centre, which after all, is where it all began. The one on the corner of Nieuwe Spiegelstraat and Keizersgracht is rumoured to be the most fertile.

Retail and other

Adonis

Warmoesstraat 92, 1012 JH Phone **627 2959**
Web **www.mantoman-adonis.com**
Sex shop with large-screen video and a very popular darkroom (and private cabins) in the back. Popular with all ages. **Open** Monday-Thursday 1000-0100. Friday-Saturday 1000-0300. Sunday 1100-0200

Alfa Blue

Nieuwendijk 26, 1012 ML Phone **627 1664**
Make the train journey go a bit more pleasantly by nipping into this place – on the shopping strip close to Centraal Station – and known to be stockists of a big selection of chubbies and chasers magazines and videos. **Open** Sunday-Thursday 0900-0000. Friday-Saturday 0900-0200

American Book Centre

Kalverstraat 185, 1012 XC Phone **625 5537**
A large bookstore with English-language books in the basement. **Open** Monday-Saturday 1000-2000. Sunday 1100-1900

Black Body

Lijnbaansgracht 292, 1017 RM Phone **626 2553**
E-mail **welcome@blackbody.nl** Web **www.blackbody.nl**
Large specialised leather and rubber collection. **Open** Monday-Friday 1000-1830. Saturday 1100-1800

The Bronx

Kerkstraat 53-55, 1017 GC Phone **623 1548**
Well-known sex shop attached to and owned by the Aero Hotel (same owners as the Camp Café) with video theatre in the back of the shop plus private cabins. Worth popping in just for the experience. Cinema ticket valid all day. **Open** Monday-Sunday 1200-0000

Cuts and Curls

Korte Leidsedwarsstraat 74, 1017 RD Phone **624 6881**
Web **www.cutsandcurls.com**
A hairdressing salon with an atmosphere and interior like you have never experienced. Three remarkable professionals who work without appointments – just walk in and check out the possibilities. **Open** Monday-Wednesday 1000-2000. Thursday 1000-2100. Friday 1000-1900. Saturday 1000-1630

Demask

Zeedijk 64, 1012 MB Phone **620 5603**
One of the world's premier leather and rubber fetish shops, which started life in good old England and now has several European branches. You can pick up everything here from club gear, home erotica and compilation CDs to gynaecological chairs. Eclectic? Oh yes. **Open** Monday-Saturday 1000-1900. Sunday 1200-1700

Drake's

Damrak 61, 1012 LM Phone **627 9544**
The sex shop part of Drake's Guest House (see 'Accommodation' listings) with a very cruisy cinema at the back of the store. The shop sells a large range of books, magazines, videos, bits and bobs and leather accessories. Upstairs you'll find 40-channel video cabins – with added ventilation – and a large-screen cinema showing the gay porn. **Open** Monday-Sunday 0900-0200

Flightbrokers

Lange Leidsedwarsstraat 96, 1017 NM Phone **420 2814**
E-mail **info@flightbrokers.nl** Web **www.flightbrokers.nl**
Travel agents with internet access. **Open** Monday-Friday 0900-2000. Saturday 1000-1700

Gay Krant Travel Service

Kloveniersburgwal 40, 1012 CW Phone **421 0000**
E-mail **travel@gaykrant.nl** Web **www.gaykrant.nl**
Travel agent that can arrange flights and accommodation around the world. Also, De Gay Krant shop. **Open** Monday 1400-1800. Tuesday-Friday 1000-1800. Saturday 1000-1600

Intermale

Spuisstraat 251, 1012 VR Phone **625 0009**
Exclusively gay and gay-related literature of all kinds and several different languages, including English. Also a good stock of non-porno videos. **Open** Monday-Saturday 1000-1800. Thursday until 2100

Man Talk
Reguliersdwarsstraat 39, 1017 BK Phone **627 2525**
Underwear and swimwear. **Open** Monday-Saturday 1000-1800

Mister B
Warmoesstraat 89, 1012 HZ Phone **422 0003**
E-mail **info@misterb.com** Web **www.misterb.com**
Leather, rubber, piercings etc. **Open** Monday-Friday 1000-1830. Saturday 1100-1800. Sunday 1300-1800

RoB
Weteringsschans 253, 1017 XJ Phone **625 4686**
E-mail **info@rob.nl** Web **www.rob.nl**
Home of the world-famous leather 'tailors', established for over 25 years. Usually RoB are the sponsors of the massive MegaTrash weekends as well as the Trash events. Always come in here to find out the latest information on the underground or irregular leather parties. **Open** Monday-Wednesday, Friday 1100-1900. Thursday 1100-2000. Saturday 1100-1800

RoB Accessories
Warmoesstraat 32, 1012 JE Phone **420 8548**
The second RoB shop, specializing in leather accessories such as hats, cockrings, belts and so on. **Open** Monday-Friday 1300-1900. Saturday 1200-1800. Sunday 1300-1800

Robin and Rik Leermakers
Runstraat 30, 1016 GK Phone **628 8924**
A small but well-respected company that has gained a well-deserved name for the absolute quality of their handmade own-label leather col-

www.malexpress.co.uk

lection. **Open** Monday 1300-1830. Tuesday-Saturday 1100-1830.

Le Salon

Nieuwendijk 20-22, 1012 ML Phone **622 6565**
Well-established store with video cabins and peep shows and one of the largest selections of porn videos and magazines in Holland. **Open** Monday-Saturday 0900-0000. Sunday 1200-0000

De Stringslip

Reguliersdwarsstraat 59, 1017 BK Phone **638 1143**
Web **www.stringslip.com**
Well-known men's underwear store, located just behind the Flower Market. In addition to its wide range of strings and lingerie you'll find swimwear; designer-label T-shirts, bodies and shorts; a collection of leather, rubber and SM accessories; some of the hottest DVDs, videos, magazines and albums as well as a variety of sex toys and souvenirs. They also sell party tickets, condoms, lube, poppers and a myriad of associated accoutrements. **Open** Monday-Saturday 1200-2100. Sunday 1400-2100

Vrolijk

Paleisstraat 135, 1012 ZL Phone **623 5142** **Web www.vrolijk.nl**
This is the largest gay and lesbian bookstore in the country. It's based behind the Queen's Palace and consists of two floors full of a wide range of books, both new and second-hand. Vrolijk also stocks DVDs, videos, postcards and miscellaneous gadgets (including Homonopolis – a gay Dutch version of Monopoly!). Open Monday 1100-1800. Tuesday-Friday 1000-1800 (except Thursday until 2100). Saturday 1000-1700

www.gaytimes.co.uk

Escorts and studios

There is a modest escort scene available in the city. Though remember, if sex is your objective, you might be cheaper hiring the services of a rent boy. Still, escorts come in various shapes (and sizes!) and will probably be that little bit more attentive and attractive. Take your pick from any of these 24-hour-a-day agencies: **AA Boys** (675 5750); **Call Boys** (679 5098); **City Boys** (400 4455); **Home Escorts** (662 3142); **Michaels Boys Escorts** (618 1824 and www.michaelsboysescorts.com).

If you fancy a bit of what you first tried on your hol's then **People Male Escorts** (662 9990 and www.peoplemale.com) is one of the city's most professional agencies who specialise in going that little bit further and who are happy to make international calls. View the site and take your pick from the comfort of your own armchair.

Then there are the studios where, rather than them coming to you, you go to them. **The Boys** at Amstel 140 (622 8036), for instance, with a bar and boys in one convenient spot, which is open Sunday to Thursday from 1700 to 0300 and Friday to Saturday from 1700 to 0400. Like Why Not (see 'Bars') on the same street, **Boysclub21** at Spuistraat 21 (622 8828) is another House of Boys that has become very well established over the years. Run by a team of straight brothers, Boysclub 21 is open Sunday to Thursday from 1200 until 0200 and Friday to Saturday from

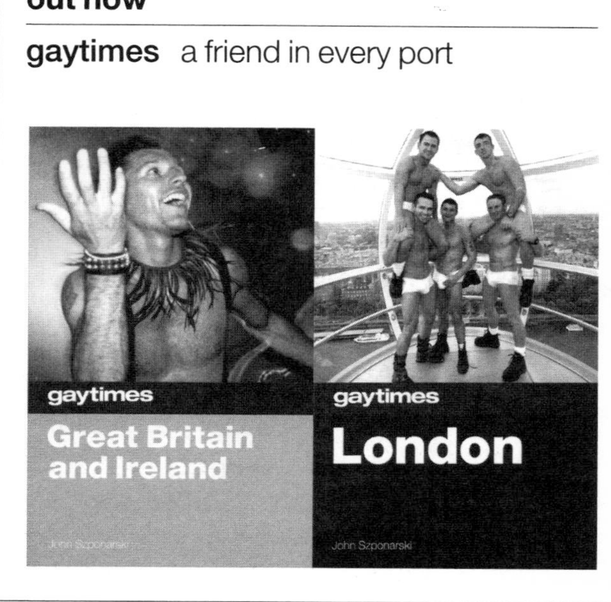

1200 to 0300. Down the road from there, at Spuistraat 44B, is **Club Boys for Men** (638 1512 and www.xs4all.nl/boys4men), which offers a discreet and welcoming atmosphere with the added bonus of an S&M cellar that is also available for private hire. The club is open Monday to Friday from 1200 to 0200 and Saturday to Sunday from 1500 to 0200. Finally, why not try it at **Try It**, a basement venue that lies out of the city centre at Kuiperstraat 86 (662 7091) and is open daily from 1300 until 2400.

Maps

NIEUWE WESTERDOK STR
DE RUIJTER
Centraal Station
STATIONSPLEIN
PRINS HENDRIKKADE
Nederlands Centrum voor Ambachten
Lutherse Kerk
HEKELVELD
NIEUWEZIJDS VOORBURGWAL
DAMRAK
Damrak
WARMOESSTRAAT
CENTRUM
Beurs van Berlage
BEURSSTRAAT
Museum Amstelkring
Oude Kerk
Nieuwe Kerk
SPUISTRAAT
Torensluis
Theatermuseum
RAADHUISSTRAAT
Magna Plaza
Koninklijk Paleis
National Monument
PALEISSTRAAT
Madame Tussaud Scenerama
Hash Marihuana Museum
De Waag
Star Hofje
Zon's Hofje
Noorder Kerk
Huis met de Hoofden
Claes Claesz Hofje
JORDAAN
Kattensloot
Kostverlorenvaart
NASSAUKADE
MARNIXSTRAAT
MARNIXPLEIN
FREDERIK HENDRIKSTRAAT
Singelgracht
Anne Frankhuis
Westerkerk
ROZENGRACHT
Suikerhof
BERENSTRAAT
WOLVENSTRAAT
Shaffy Theater
ELANDSGRACHT
Lijnbaansgracht
Looier Kunst en Antiekcentrum
Openbare Bibliotheek
Bijbels Museum
Bernadus
Metz & Co
Paleis van Justitie
Melkweg
De la Mar Theater
Stadsschouwburg
NIEUWEZIJDS VOORBURGWAL
ROKIN
Amsterdams Historisch Museum
Stadhuis (City Hall)
St Agnietenkapel
Oostindisch Huis
Trippe-huis
KLOVENIERSBURGWAL
ST ANTONIESBREESTRAAT
Zuider Kerk
Allard Pierson Museum
Universiteit
Museum Het Rembrandthuis
Universiteit van Amsterdam
Theater School
Krijtberg
KONINGSPLEIN
Munttoren
Bloemenmarkt
AMSTEL
Stadhuis en Operagebouw
Tuschinski Theater
BLAUWBR
Museum Willet Holthuysen
Six Collection
VIJZELSTRAAT
Museum Fodor
Museum Van Loon
UTRECHTSESTRAAT
Amstelkerk
1e CONSTANTIJN HUYGENSSTRAAT
OVERTOOM
PLANTSOEN
STADHOUDERSKADE
WETERINGSCHANS
Nederlands Filmmuseum
HOBBEMASTRAAT
Rijksmuseum
VIJZELGRACHT
Vondelpark
VAN BAERLESTRAAT
Coster Diamonds
Van Gogh Museum
HOBBEMA STR
Stedelijk Museum
MUSEUM PLEIN
MUSEUMSTRAAT
KLM Air Terminal
Museum Zuiderbad
WILLEMSPARKWEG
Heineken Brouwerij
Singelgracht
Nederlandse Bank
WESTEINDE
STADHOUDERSKADE

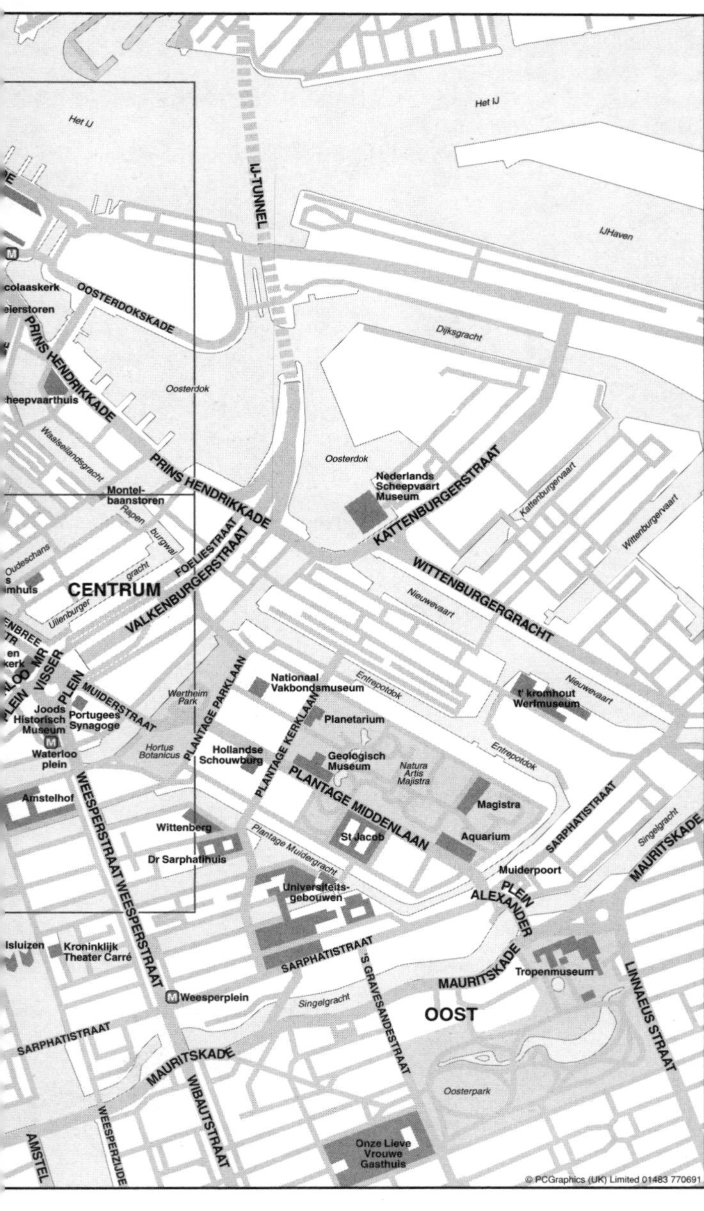
Het IJ
IJ-TUNNEL
IJHaven
Dijksgracht
OOSTERDOKSKADE
PRINS HENDRIKKADE
Oosterdok
Nederlands Scheepvaart Museum
KATTENBURGERSTRAAT
Kattenburgervaart
Wittenburgervaart
WITTENBURGERGRACHT
Nieuwevaart
Montelbaanstoren
CENTRUM
VALKENBURGERSTRAAT
FOELIESTRAAT
Entrepotdok
Nationaal Vakbondsmuseum
Planetarium
t' kromhout Werfmuseum
MUIDERSTRAAT
Joods Historisch Museum
Portugees Synagoge
Waterloo plein
Wertheim Park
Hortus Botanicus
PLANTAGE PARKLAAN
Hollandse Schouwburg
PLANTAGE KERKLAAN
Geologisch Museum
Natura Artis Majistra
PLANTAGE MIDDENLAAN
Magistra
Aquarium
St Jacob
Amstelhof
Wittenberg
Dr Sarphatihuis
Plantage Muidergracht
Universiteits-gebouwen
Muiderpoort
ALEXANDER PLEIN
SARPHATISTRAAT
Singelgracht
MAURITSKADE
WEESPERSTRAAT
Kroninklijk Theater Carré
Tropenmuseum
LINNAEUS STRAAT
'S GRAVESANDESTRAAT
Weesperplein
OOST
Oosterpark
WIBAUTSTRAAT
WEESPERZIJDE
AMSTEL
Onze Lieve Vrouwe Gasthuis
© PCGraphics (UK) Limited 01483 770691

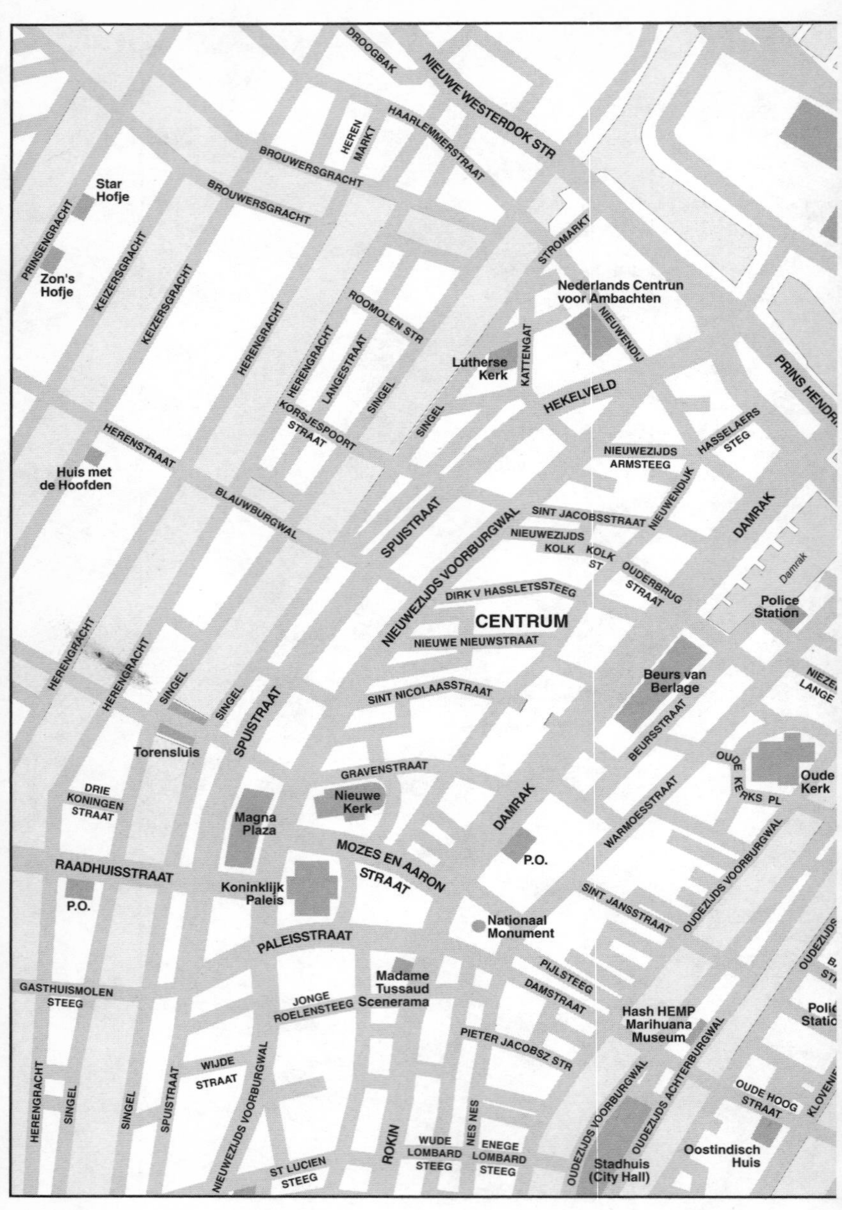

DROOGBAK
NIEUWE WESTERDOK STR
HAARLEMMERSTRAAT
HEREN MARKT
BROUWERSGRACHT
BROUWERSGRACHT
Star Hofje
PRINSENGRACHT
Zon's Hofje
KEIZERSGRACHT
KEIZERSGRACHT
HERENGRACHT
HERENGRACHT
LANGESTRAAT
ROOMOLEN STR
SINGEL
SINGEL
STROMARKT
Nederlands Centrun voor Ambachten
NIEUWENDIJ
Lutherse Kerk
KATTENGAT
HEKELVELD
PRINS HENDR
KORSJESPOORT STRAAT
HERENSTRAAT
Huis met de Hoofden
BLAUWBURGWAL
SPUISTRAAT
NIEUWEZIJDS ARMSTEEG
HASSELAERS STEG
NIEUWENDIJK
DAMRAK
SINT JACOBSSTRAAT
NIEUWEZIJDS KOLK
KOLK ST
OUDERBRUG STRAAT
Damrak
Police Station
NIEUWEZIJDS VOORBURGWAL
DIRK V HASSLETSSTEEG
CENTRUM
NIEUWE NIEUWSTRAAT
HERENGRACHT
HERENGRACHT
SINGEL
SINGEL
SPUISTRAAT
SINT NICOLAASSTRAAT
Beurs van Berlage
BEURSSTRAAT
NIEZE LANGE
Torensluis
GRAVENSTRAAT
OUDE KERKS PL
Oude Kerk
DRIE KONINGEN STRAAT
Nieuwe Kerk
Magna Plaza
DAMRAK
WARMOESSTRAAT
MOZES EN AARON STRAAT
P.O.
RAADHUISSTRAAT
P.O.
Koninklijk Paleis
SINT JANSSTRAAT
OUDEZIJDS VOORBURGWAL
Nationaal Monument
PALEISSTRAAT
PIJLSTEEG
DAMSTRAAT
Madame Tussaud Scenerama
GASTHUISMOLEN STEEG
JONGE ROELENSTEEG
Hash HEMP Marihuana Museum
PIETER JACOBSZ STR
WIJDE STRAAT
HERENGRACHT
SINGEL
SINGEL
SPUISTRAAT
NIEUWEZIJDS VOORBURGWAL
ROKIN
NES NES
WUDE LOMBARD STEEG
ENEGE LOMBARD STEEG
OUDEZIJDS VOORBURGWAL
OUDEZIJDS ACHTERBURGWAL
OUDE HOOG STRAAT
Stadhuis (City Hall)
Oostindisch Huis
ST LUCIEN STEEG

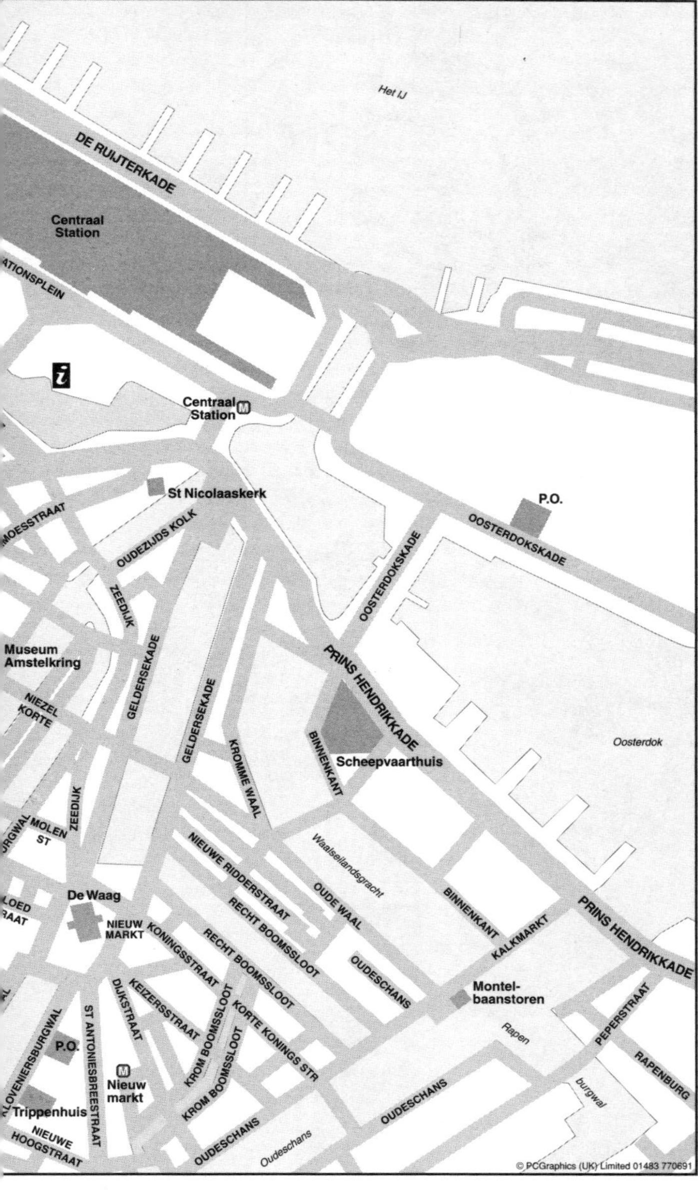
Het IJ
DE RUIJTERKADE
Centraal Station
STATIONSPLEIN
Centraal Station
St Nicolaaskerk
P.O.
OOSTERDOKSKADE
OOSTERDOKSKADE
OUDEZIJDS KOLK
ZEEDIJK
Museum Amstelkring
GELDERSEKADE
GELDERSEKADE
PRINS HENDRIKKADE
BINNENKANT
Scheepvaarthuis
KROMME WAAL
Oosterdok
NIEZEL
KORTE
ZEEDIJK
MOLEN ST
NIEUWE RIDDERSTRAAT
Waalseilandsgracht
OUDE WAAL
RECHT BOOMSSLOOT
RECHT BOOMSSLOOT
BINNENKANT
KALKMARKT
PRINS HENDRIKKADE
De Waag
NIEUW MARKT
KONINGSSTRAAT
OUDESCHANS
Montelbaanstoren
DIJKSTRAAT
KEIZERSSTRAAT
KORTE KONINGS STR
KROM BOOMSSLOOT
KROM BOOMSSLOOT
Rapen
PEPERSTRAAT
RAPENBURG
burgwal
KLOVENIERSBURGWAL
P.O.
ST ANTONIESBREESTRAAT
Nieuw markt
Trippenhuis
NIEUWE HOOGSTRAAT
OUDESCHANS
OUDESCHANS
Oudeschans
© PCGraphics (UK) Limited 01483 770691

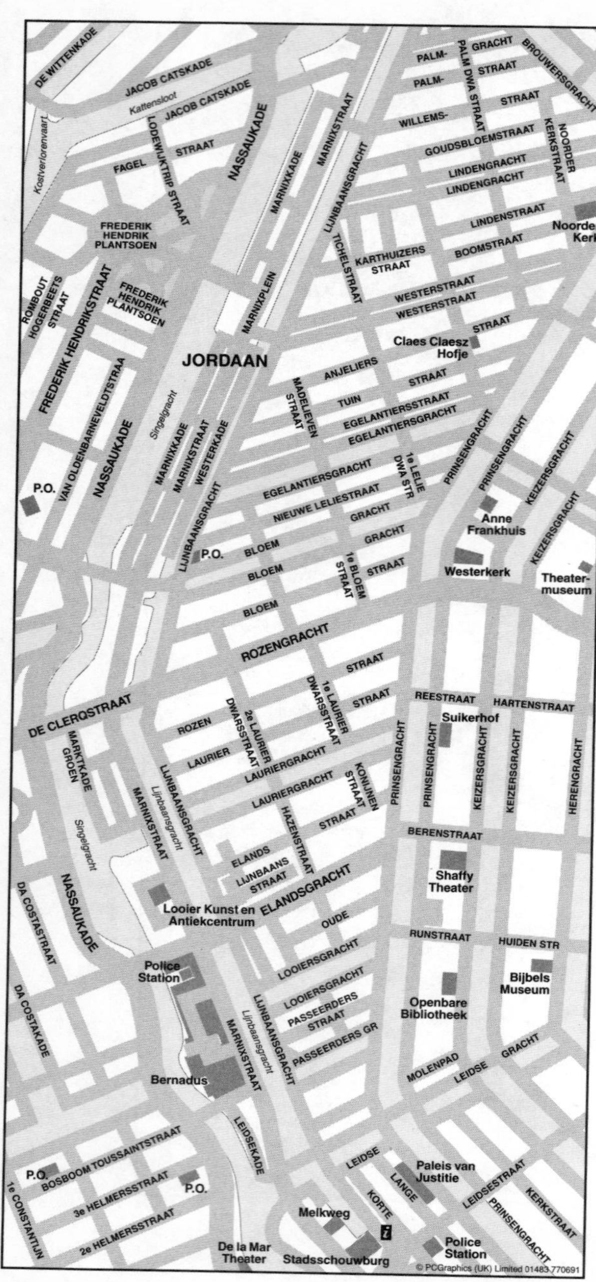
DE WITTENKADE
JACOB CATSKADE
Kattensloot
JACOB CATSKADE
Kostverlorenvaart
LODEWIJKTRIP STRAAT
FAGEL
STRAAT
NASSAUKADE
MARNIXKADE
MARNIXSTRAAT
LIJNBAANSGRACHT
PALM-
GRACHT
PALM DWA STRAAT
BROUWERSGRACHT
PALM-
STRAAT
WILLEMS-
STRAAT
GOUDSBLOEMSTRAAT
KERKSTRAAT
NOORDER
LINDENGRACHT
LINDENGRACHT
LINDENSTRAAT
Noorder Kerk
FREDERIK HENDRIK PLANTSOEN
TICHELSTRAAT
KARTHUIZERS STRAAT
BOOMSTRAAT
ROMBOUT HOGERBEETS STRAAT
FREDERIK HENDRIKSTRAAT
FREDERIK HENDRIK PLANTSOEN
MARNIXPLEIN
WESTERSTRAAT
WESTERSTRAAT
STRAAT
Claes Claesz Hofje
JORDAAN
ANJELIERS
STRAAT
MADELIEVEN STRAAT
TUIN
EGELANTIERSSTRAAT
EGELANTIERSGRACHT
Singelgracht
VAN OLDENBARNEVELDTSTRAAT
NASSAUKADE
MARNIXKADE
MARNIXSTRAAT
WESTERKADE
PRINSENGRACHT
PRINSENGRACHT
KEIZERSGRACHT
1e LELIE DWA STR
EGELANTIERSGRACHT
P.O.
LIJNBAANSGRACHT
EGELANTIERSGRACHT
NIEUWE LELIESTRAAT
GRACHT
KEIZERSGRACHT
Anne Frankhuis
GRACHT
P.O.
BLOEM
1e BLOEM STRAAT
STRAAT
Westerkerk
Theater-museum
BLOEM
BLOEM
ROZENGRACHT
STRAAT
DE CLERQSTRAAT
1e LAURIER DWARSSTRAAT
STRAAT
REESTRAAT
HARTENSTRAAT
Suikerhof
ROZEN
2e LAURIER DWARSSTRAAT
MARKTKADE GROEN
LAURIER
LAURIERGRACHT
LAURIERGRACHT
KONIJNEN STRAAT
PRINSENGRACHT
PRINSENGRACHT
KEIZERSGRACHT
KEIZERSGRACHT
HERENGRACHT
LIJNBAANSGRACHT
MARNIXSTRAAT
Lijnbaansgracht
Singelgracht
HAZENSTRAAT
STRAAT
BERENSTRAAT
ELANDS
LIJNBAANS STRAAT
ELANDSGRACHT
Shaffy Theater
DA COSTASTRAAT
NASSAUKADE
Looier Kunst en Antiekcentrum
OUDE
RUNSTRAAT
HUIDEN STR
LOOIERSGRACHT
Police Station
Bijbels Museum
DA COSTAKADE
LOOIERSGRACHT
PASSEERDERS STRAAT
Openbare Bibliotheek
LIJNBAANSGRACHT
Lijnbaansgracht
MARNIXSTRAAT
PASSEERDERS GR
MOLENPAD
LEIDSE
GRACHT
Bernadus
LEIDSEKADE
BOSBOOM TOUSSAINTSTRAAT
P.O.
LEIDSE
Paleis van Justitie
LANGE
LEIDSESTRAAT
KERKSTRAAT
PRINSENGRACHT
P.O.
1e CONSTANTIJN
3e HELMERSSTRAAT
KORTE
Melkweg
2e HELMERSSTRAAT
De la Mar Theater
Stadsschouwburg
Police Station
© PCGraphics (UK) Limited 01483 770691

Notes

Notes

Notes

Notes

Notes

Notes

Notes

Notes